Consensus

Copyright 2006 Marion Baumgart dos Santos

All rights reserved. No part of this publication may be reproduced, stored in a retrieval system, or transmitted in any form or by any means, electronic, mechanical, photocopying, recording or otherwise, without prior permission from the publishers.

Published by
Kachere Series
P.O. Box 1037, Zomba, Malawi
ISBN 99908-76-72-X (Kachere Texts no. 27)

Represented outside Africa by
African Books Collective, Oxford (orders@africanbookscollective.com)
Michigan State University Press, East Lansing (msupress@msu.edu)

Layout: Marion Baumgart dos Santos
Cover Design: Mercy Chilunga and Marion Baumgart dos Santos
The printing of this book was funded by the GTZ – Combating Gender Based Violence Project.

Printed in Malawi by Montfort Media, P.O. Box 280, Balaka

Consensus

Combating Gender Based Violence through Islam, Tradition and Law

Marion Baumgart dos Santos

Kachere Texts no. 27

Kachere Series

Zomba

2006

Kachere Series
P.O. Box 1037, Zomba, Malawi
kachere@globemw.net
www.sdnp.org.mw/kachereseries/

This book is part of the Kachere Series, a range of books on religion, culture, and society from Malawi. Other Kachere titles so far are:

Maria Saur et. al., *Nkhanza: Listening to People's Voices*
WLSA, *In Search of Justice: Women and the Administration of Justice in Malawi*
Seodi White et.al., *Dispossessing the Widow: Gender Based Violence in Malawi*
Rachel Nyagondwe Fielder, *Coming of Age: A Christianized Initiation among Women in Southern Malawi*
Janet Y. Kholowa and Klaus Fiedler, *In the Beginning God Created them Equal*
Martin Ott et. al., *The Power of the Vote: Malawi 2004 Parliamentary and Presidential Elections*
Bodo Immink et. al., *From Freedom to Empowerment: Ten Years of Democratisation in Malawi*
Fulata Moyo and Martin Ott (eds.) *Christianity and the Environment: Care for what you have been Given*
Rachel Nyagondwe Banda, *Women of the Bible and Culture: Baptist Convention Women in Southern Malawi*
David S Bone (ed.) *Malawi's Muslims: Historical Perspectives*
James N Amanze, *African Traditional Religion in Malawi: The Case of the Bimbi Cult*

The Kachere Series is the publications arm of the Department of Theology and Religious Studies of the University of Malawi

Series Editors: J.C. Chakanza, F.L. Chingota, Klaus Fiedler, P.A. Kalilombe, S. Mahomad, Chimwemwe Katumbi

Content

Acknowledgements	6
Preface	7
Remarks from the Institutions	
Judiciary	11
Muslim Association of Malawi	12
The Partners	
Muslim Association of Malawi	13
The GTZ-Lekani Nkhanza Project	16
The Mangochi Network against gender based violence	18
The Dialogue Process	19
Transcriptions of Dialogues	
Gender roles in marriage and society	21
Expectations and consequences of a marriage	32
Extra-marital affairs	41
Spousal battery - Correctional beating	51
Denied Sex, Forced Sex and Rape	61
Rejection and Desertion	72
Divorce and Property	85
Property Grabbing	103
Reference	114

Acknowledgements

The author's responsibility for the content of this booklet is very limited - her main task being to compile and edit the contributions of several individuals representing different institutions. We would like to thank all of them; without their valuable input, the public dialogues would not have been the success that they were.

The assistance of the following institutions and their representatives (in alphabetical order) is acknowledged:

Judiciary
Dorothy nyaKamanga Kaunda, High Court; and Esme Tembenu, magistrate – panelists.

Lekani Nkhanza Project
Sindisiwe Kabwila, transcription and translation; Venencia Kabwila, conceptualization and facilitation; Grace Nhlema, organization and administration.

Mangochi Network against Gender Based Violence
The network has approximately 20 members from different institutions; all of them, sometimes even their family members and friends, contributed in one way or another to the panel discussions. Thank you very much. We would like to mention particularly Mrs. Delezina Gomiwa, magistrate, who was co-responsible for the conceptualization and organization of the whole event.

Muslim Association of Malawi
Sheikh Mussa Idrissa – conceptualization, organization and panelist; Sheikh Salmin Omar, Sheikh Abdurahman Morice – panellists, Sheikh Saidi Jambo – facilitator.

Traditional Authorities
T/A Chowe – conceptualization, organization and panelist; T/A Bwananyambi; T/A Chimwala; Senior Chief Jalassi; T/A Katuli; T/A Makanjira, T/A Mponda; T/A Namavi; T/A Nankumba – panellists.

Preface

This booklet is the result of eighteen months' cooperation between the Muslim Association of Malawi, the GTZ Combating Gender Based Violence Project, the Mangochi Network against Gender Based Violence and the GTZ Consultancy Unit "Islam and Technical Cooperation in Africa". It is based on nine public dialogues that took place in all the nine T/As of Mangochi in the period January – July 2005 involving between 800 and 1500 participants per dialogue.

This cooperation began with research carried out in Mangochi District on the current and potential roles of the Muslim Community in Mangochi, Malawi, in combating gender based violence. An important finding of this study was that, while governmental and non-governmental organizations also have a stake in combating gender based violence, the main actors in preventing and resolving *nkhanza*[1] cases are currently the chiefs, group village headmen and T/As. However, the sheiks (who are respected as moral authorities and could, therefore, contribute to the prevention of gender based violence through sensitization) are not involved. This, the research showed, was primarily because of their low literacy levels and, consequently, their limited understanding of the teachings of the Qur'an and their restricted capacity to interpret its verses. On the other hand, the potential for them to contribute was highly appreciated by all stakeholders involved as well as by the Muslim Association and the sheikhs themselves.

To empower them, as religious leaders, to contribute to eradicating nkhanza in line with human rights, ways of familiarizing the sheikhs within an oral culture had to be found. The best way that people learn in an oral culture is when they listen, watch, sing or play. But in this case, listening to Islamic teachings would not have been enough

---

[1] Studies conducted by the Project revealed that the western notion of violence does not correspond with the Chichewa translation, which is "nkhanza". While the western term gives physical harm more emphasis, the Malawian perception is embedded in a broader understanding of violence. People perceive psychological cruelty, structural violence and various other forms of abuse as seriously as physical harm. With regard to those findings, we will refer to the local understanding of "nkhanza" throughout the book.

because the behaviour of people is not only guided by religious principles, but also by traditional values and customs and the laws of the county. It was therefore decided to bring together representatives from the three institutions – Islam, tradition and law – to discuss issues of gender based violence in a public setting. Contrary to what usually happens at public debates, where participants try to convince the audience that they have the better arguments, it was decided to hold public dialogues rather than debates. The focus of these would be on the elaboration of a **common ground** between the approaches and opinions of the three institutions.

We were well aware that there are differences in the points of view of the three institutions, as well as prejudgements of the other institution(s). For example, traditional and religious leaders sometimes consider the human rights approach as something contrary to their customs; while on the other hand, there are several human rights activists and religious leaders who regard tradition as something that has to be overcome during the process of modernisation, Christianisation or Islamization. Islam and sharia are often falsely regarded as contradictory to human rights, especially when it comes to women's rights.

The Malawian law, Islam and traditions have set rules to regulate human behaviour. Lawyers and Parliament have produced the Malawian Constitution, Islam has the sharia, and traditions are passed orally from one generation to the other. But all of these rule-based systems are open to interpretation or change. In fact only about 80 of the Koran's 6,000 verses lay down rules of public law, and not many of these have much application in the modern world. Much of what is loosely called *sharia* derives from other sources: the *sunna* (the teachings of the prophet); the *ijma* (the consensus of religious scholars); and the *qiyas* (legal reasoning). So there is ample room for interpretation (what Muslims call *ijtihad*). Even some explicit laws laid down in the Koran are routinely circumvented by Islamic judges.

The same is true of the Malawian Constitution. While it lays down guidelines, it is up to judges to interpret these and adapt them to the facts of the case they are handling at the time.

And last but not least, over the previous centuries, Malawian traditions have proved their capacity to adapt themselves to new circumstances and conditions. If they weren't able to do so, they would not remain such an important and relevant tool in guiding people's behaviour today.

So, the challenge for this cooperation was to establish an environment where participants would be able to interpret their own rule system towards reaching consensus with each of the other two systems. Our assumption was that it is much easier to reach consensus when dealing with daily issues and problems than with theoretical or theological questions. We therefore decided that participants should present their institution's point of view regarding concrete issues like "divorce and property" or "spousal battery" and not on general questions like "women's rights". At the end of the discussions, the audience should have a clear understanding of the common ground between the three institutions and should go home with possible solutions for their daily problems.

In the following pages, we begin with a short background of the partners involved in the panel discussion. Next, we focus on the dialogue methodology used. The bulk of the report is taken up with the contributions of the panellists on the different issues of *nkhanza*. To make the transcriptions more reader-friendly, these have been condensed a little to avoid repetitions that occur naturally in the spoken language. We also provide a brief introduction to the issue dealt with in that particular chapter and a conclusion at its end.

We have deliberately abstained from evaluating the contributions of the panellists. It is not our task to judge if the statements are a progressive or regressive interpretation of the law, Islam or tradition, or how the individual points of view fit into the current national or international discussions about women's rights, interpretations of the Qur'an or any similar debate. Readers may come up with their own opinions or conclusions, which may differ according to their individual and cultural background.

During a study that was concluded at the beginning of the Project, it was found that violence in all its forms (such as physical or verbal abuse) is regarded within Malawi as an acceptable method of resolving conflict, not only within the family, but also within hospitals, prisons, schools and between members of different political parties. Exchanging opinions on controversial matters in a peaceful and respectful way, where partners might come to a partial agreement but accept that, even after lengthy dialogue there might still be some differences, is a process that should be further encouraged within Malawi.

We hope that the panel discussions have not only contributed to the fight against gender based violence, but that they will serve also as a role model for peaceful and successful conflict resolution, thereby contributing to the development of democracy in Malawi.

Remarks from the Institutions

Judiciary

The Mission statement of the Judiciary is: "To provide independent and impartial justice and judicial services that are efficient and that earn the respect, trust and confidence of the society".

This mission statement demonstrates that the key role of the Judiciary is to protect, promote and uphold the rule of law, democracy and human rights as enshrined in the Constitution. The role of the Judiciary is more pronounced in a constitutional democracy and democratization entails transformation in institutional arrangements and perspectives to which the Judiciary must respond. The influence of the Judiciary on democracy, governance, human rights and social, political and economic development continues to expand as it adapts responsively to developments in these areas.

The community meetings that were carried out under this project focused on many issues and problems pertaining to the law, social/traditional/cultural practices and the Qur'an, which have helped to enrich and inform our ideas on the issues of gender based violence. We have come to appreciate that the nature of society is inherently plural and characterized by diversity with historical, religious, economic and gender variables affecting people's values and norms. As a result of participating in this project any misunderstandings or misperceptions that we might have had on gender based violence and the Islamic teachings have been clarified (if not totally disappeared). The community meetings show that there is much in common between the three sectors that calls for closer collaboration in order to improve access to justice for all people in Malawi. One major area of agreement among us is the need to uphold justice. It is also clear that there are several primary and formal systems and structures in society through which to effect justice. The real challenge now lies in the ability of the primary and formal justice structures to deliver justice without discrimination, especially with regard to gender.

Muslim Association of Malawi

For the last few months, panel discussions have been conducted in all nine traditional authorities in the district and I would like to explain here that the programme has exposed glaring issues which have been kept under cover for a long time. Sometimes this covering up has been on purpose while at times it has been due to ignorance. Yet they have a very negative impact not only to the society but even on the Islamic religion. Indeed chiefs who participated in the panel discussions would agree with me that they were an eye opener for all of us, and the general public on the magnitude of gender based violence in our social constructions.

As a religious leader, and a Sheikh in particular, I would like to admit that the programme exposed our weaknesses in such a way that we seem to sit and remain silent on issues or matters which are clear in both the Qur'an and Sunnah. Therefore, the programme has made us rethink our position and responsibility towards eliminating social ills and building a just society.

On behalf of the Muslim Association of Malawi (MAM), and indeed on my own behalf, allow me to express my sincere appreciation to GTZ for recognising MAM as a partner in this project. Surely, your gesture does not only symbolize a spirit of networking and collaboration but also that GTZ is not here with a hidden agenda of destroying Islamic religion and the Yao culture in the district under the veil of communal assistance of development programmes (as other organizations do).

At this point, I would like to encourage my fellow religious leaders, traditional leaders, and the general public to work together in combating gender based violence in the district. Let us take the lessons learned in our panel discussions as our references in issues of gender and human rights, since there is no religion or culture, which promotes gender in-balance and violence. Let Mangochi be a gender based violence free area.

The Partners

Muslim Association of Malawi

In Malawi, 12.8% of the population follows Islam, 79.9% are Christians and 7.3% follow traditional African religions, Hinduism or no religion. Most Muslims live in the district of Mangochi at Lake Malawi.

Islam came to Malawi through several routes. It was introduced to the country through the Jumbes, local rulers who represented the Sultan of Zanzibar and ruled along the coast of Lake Nyasa (now Lake Malawi) for most of the second half of the 19th century. During the same period, the Yao, an ethnic group that was until then based in Mozambique, migrated to the southern tip of the lake, bringing Islam with them. Additionally, as Christianity spread during the period of British colonization, adopting Islam was seen as a means of resisting colonization.

With the independence of Malawi in 1964 a new generation of Muslims began to emerge. It encompassed those who have obtained their training in foreign funded schools in Malawi and/or subsequently abroad, thus having established links with the wider Muslim world. While clearly being more conscious of the wider Muslim world they are also committed to their Malawian identity.

Most of the Yao Muslims are Sunni who adhere to the Shafi School of Islamic jurisprudence. However, among them are three factions. The first of these evolved as a result of traditional *Madrassa*[2] education and interaction with local customs. The second, often closely associated with the first, developed through the activities of the Sufi brotherhoods (*turuq*). Those who have been exposed to contemporary education and had overseas experience represent the third group. The challenge facing these groups was to find a common denominator. From time to time they have experienced strong tensions. Today, that tension is more marked between the younger generation of highly educated Muslims with a wider vision for the

---

[2] Qur'anic school

community and those that have maintained the more traditional Malawi Muslim way of life.

The Muslim Association of Malawi is the umbrella organization of all Muslims in Malawi. Malawian Muslims founded it in 1947. The association coordinates the activities of the Muslim community of Malawi and the various Muslim organizations, which sprang up recently in Malawi. One of the goals of MAM is to unite the various Muslim communities in Malawi into one entity and to demolish the differences, which arise due to the various factions.

The Muslim Association is an hierarchical organization with branch offices reaching into the various districts. Its chairman is the leader of all Muslims in Malawi. At Mangochi district, a sheikh represents all Muslims of Mangochi. In each Traditional Authority (T/A), there is a chairman of the Muslim Association. Each TA-branch has a Vice Chairman, a Secretary, a Vice Secretary, a Treasurer, a Vice Treasurer, and a Messenger.

Larger villages have a "highest Sheikh", who ought to be in direct contact with the Muslim Association's chairmen in the T/As and therefore be linked to the MAM and the broader Muslim community of Malawi. The villagers suggest the highest Sheikh of a village and the Village Headman/woman confirms his appointment. He has the authority to instruct the other Sheikhs and *Mu'allimus*[3]. It is he who performs the most important parts of ceremonies, such as funerals, and who is in charge of the mosque. However, this structure does not appear in every village. Small settlements may not have more than one Sheikh. In some villages, the authority of the Sheikh tends to stay within a certain family, as it happens often that a Sheikh is teaching his son, who will take over from his father.

Beside the secular education system, there is an Islamic education system in the villages. The degree of Islamic education varies enormously at village level. Some of the Sheikhs just attended 3 years of *Madrassa* or private lessons at a Sheikh's house in the afternoons before becoming a Sheikh themselves. Usually, a Sheikh had a private teacher within the same or neighbouring village. The teacher then designates his pupil to be a Sheikh.

---

[3] Teacher at Madrassa

The most common way of obtaining further education for Sheikhs and other interested people is through taking private lessons with a more educated Sheikh living nearby. Usually, this is free of charge or for a small fee. However, it was reported that quite a number of Sheikhs are not well trained in translating and interpreting the holy Qur'an.

Nevertheless, there is a small and young Muslim elite rising up due to the improved accessibility of further Islamic studies. On one hand, there are Islamic teaching institutions in the nearby urban areas such as: the Mangochi Islamic Center, Munazzamat Da'wa Islamia (MDI) in Mangochi, Blantyre Islamic Mission, Linthipe Islamic Centre in Lilongwe, and Salima Islamic Centre, which offer secular and/ or Islamic education. All have opened up recently. Some of them are foreign organizations, funded by donors worldwide. On the other hand, there are organizations which give funds to poor students who want to study at these centres or even abroad. People reported of having studied in Sudan, Tanzania, Kenya, Egypt, Saudi Arabia or Kuwait. However, the possibility for financial assistance is decreasing nowadays.

The Sheikhs are mainly engaged in overseeing funerals. They are also taking care of other Islamic ceremonies, for example at Ramadan or other Islamic feasts. Furthermore, the religious authorities lead prayers and preach at mosques on Fridays. Most of the Sheikhs in the villages do not get paid for their activities. Whenever there is a funeral or any other ceremony, the Sheikhs of the neighbourhood are present. It is the norm that when a Sheikh travels to a nearby village and it is the time of Friday prayer, the Sheikh of that particular village invites the other to pray in the mosque. The Sheikhs take that as a good opportunity to confirm one's own preaching by another Sheikh, as well as to give their faith community a change. Because of this practice of "exchange of preaching" the Sheikhs are, to some extent, aware of the content of the preaching of other Sheikhs.

The Lekani Nkhanza Project

In 1998 the Ministry of Gender, Child Welfare and Community Services requested support from the German Government through GTZ for the implementation of the National Platform for Action. As a result, the long-term advisory project "Combating Gender Based Violence" was conceived. Its implementation started in February 2003 and its partners are the Ministry of Gender, Child Welfare and Community Services at policy level, and several national and local institutions and organizations. The overall purpose of the project is to improve the social and legal situation of women so that they are able to independently exercise their rights.

During research carried out at the beginning of the project, it was found out that Malawians consider as root causes for gender based violence:

- Unequal power relationship between men and women. This is not only a Malawian phenomenon but an international one. All over the world, men consider women as inferior due to the tasks they perform in the household and society. As a result, they are more vulnerable to physical violence and have less power to control resources like land, money or other valuable assets. They also have less access to education, schools and so on.
- Lack of knowledge regarding human rights and the Malawian Constitution. After the introduction of the multi-party system and the consequent propagation of democracy and human rights, many misunderstanding arise in villages. Several people understand this new freedom as an opportunity to do whatever they want – to beat others or to avoid their responsibilities towards their spouses and children – without taking into consideration the rights of others and the Malawian Constitution.
- Lack of proper communication within the couple and extended family. For example, a wife comes back late from the borehole and without asking her why, her husband starts accusing her of having been together with another man and then slaps her. On

the other hand, the husband might come home late and without listening to his explanation, his wife assumes he was out with another woman and, therefore, she locks him out.

Based on those findings, the project tries to:
- Promote gender sensitization at grassroots and district level. For example, within the last two years, approximately 300 village committees have been trained on gender issues as the first step in a longer training cycle. These village committees are made up of influential people in the villages, such as the chiefs, *anankungwi, angaliba*,[4] nurses and teachers. To train these committees, more then eighty trainers were trained.
- Increase the knowledge of human rights and the Constitution. The same target group above was also trained in human Rights and Malawian law relating to marriage, divorce and property. In addition, several campaigns where carried out with different partners like the Malawian Police, Public Affairs Committee and the panel discussions that form the substance of this book.
- Find ways to substitute violent conflict resolution mechanisms with non-violent ones. The above mentioned village committees and their trainers were also trained in mediation and conflict resolution skills. And dialogue processes like the one described in this book are also intended to serve as a role model for a non-violent way of dealing with different and sometimes challenging opinions.

The impact areas of the project are: Rumphi, Dedza, Lilongwe/Kanengo, Mangochi and Mulanje. Due to changes in German politics, the project will be phased out by December 2005.

---

[4] Men and women responsible for the initiation

The Mangochi Network against Gender Based Violence

The Mangochi Network against Gender Based Violence was founded in 1999. It is made up of approximately 25 members from different governmental, non-governmental and religious institutions like Social Welfare and Community Development, Education, Malawi Police, the Judiciary, Malawi Carer, Faith Communities and Radio Maria to mention a few. All of the network members work on a voluntary basis.

Members of the network have agreed to work together as a network for three reasons:
- All of them work in the communities where, as part of their daily work, they are confronted with the impact and effects of all forms of *nkhanza* – from spousal battery to rape, child abuse and ill-treatment of orphans. Being sensitive to social injustice, they felt it necessary to do something more then what they were able to do in their jobs alone.
- Nkanza does not happen only to 'others'; it happens within most Malawian extended families. Several members of the network were confronted within their families with incidents of nkanza. But instead of trying to resolve these problems within the family alone, they consider it a social and cultural problem to and try to combat it as such.
- They share an understanding that, through collaboration and networking, they are able to have greater impact than working in isolation in their institutions.

The network meets monthly to discuss cases that have come to their organizations, to refer them to other institutions if necessary, to update the other members of new developments within their respective organizations, and to coordinate activates in the communities. Several members of the network have been trained by the Lekani Nkhanza Project as trainers of village committees.

The Dialogue Process

Most of us know public debates, where participants usually stand for different points of view on a certain issue within a society. For example, representatives of different parties may publicly debate the reformation of a law between themselves or with their counterparts from civil society. Participants try to convince the audience of their position; they express unswerving commitment to a point of view, approach or idea. As a consequence, the atmosphere is often threatening; attacks and interruptions are made by participants and are usually permitted by the facilitator. The panellists listen in order to refute the other side's opinion and to expose faulty logic in their arguments. Questions are asked from a position of certainty. These questions are often rhetorical challenges or disguised statements.

Adopting a similar approach for our process would have substantially raised the potential for conflict and competition between the panellists and would not have suited our purpose. Instead, we wanted to establish an environment where people could feel free to exchange ideas, learn from and about each other, and come to an agreement at the end of the dialogue.

When planning for the correct environment, we had the following assumptions:
- People are more likely to have a constructive conversation when they do not attack, are not defensive and generally abstain from polarizing ways of speaking.
- Equal respect for everyone enhances trust and collaboration.
- In an affirming, exploratory, future-oriented atmosphere, people are more open to new ways of communicating.
- People learn more and relate better when they listen carefully to each other.
- When people have an enquiring attitude about others, they interact more constructively than when they speak from certainty.

Based on these assumptions, we sought to establish an environment where the task of the participants would not be to convince the audience of their position, but rather to explain it as one possibility amongst others. Therefore, there should be no need to remain unshakably committed to an approach. We hoped to create an atmosphere of safety, where the facilitators could make proposals, reach agreements on certain points and enforce clear ground rules to enhance safety and promote respectful exchange. Panellists were expected to listen to, understand and gain insight into the beliefs and concerns of the others. Questions should be asked from a position of curiosity rather than to expose weaknesses. To distinguish it from a debate, we chose to call our setting a public dialogue.

The organization of such a public dialogue required different preparation to that of a public debate:
- To guarantee ownership, the concept of the public dialogues was planed and established together with representatives from the Muslim Association, the T/As, the law, the Lekani Nkhanza project and the Mangochi network against gender based violence.
- Before every public dialogue, we held meetings with all of the panellists with the objective of:
  - Introducing the new method of discussion to them.
  - Familiarizing them with their fellow panellists and their points of view.
  - Reaching consent on the differences and possibilities for establishing a common ground
  - Agreeing the ground rules (like mutual respect for the opinion of others) with them.

During the dialogues, the facilitator's task was to make sure that:
- Participants kept to the ground rules set by themselves
- All panellists participated equally, if possible.
- Nobody tried to interrupt the others.

Transcription of the Dialogues

Gender roles in marriage and society

"A woman has to make sure her husband's stomach is fed" – "Mwamuna ndi pamimba" Malawian proverb

"I shall not lose sight of the labour of any of you who labours in My way, be it man or woman; each of you is equal to the other" (Qur'an, 3:195)

"Each member of the family shall enjoy full and equal respect and shall be protected by law against all forms of neglect, cruelty or exploitation." (Malawi Constitution 22.2)

In marriage, men and women have to perform different roles. This is an indisputable fact; nobody would dare to question it. But when we start to analyse it more in depth, several questions arise:

- What is the reason behind this division of roles?
- What are the consequences of the different roles for men and women? Can that be linked to the spread of *nkhanza*?

In order to answer these questions, let us analyse a case study:

> *Pilira was born as the 5th child of a rural family in Mangochi. She has three elder brothers and one elder sister. Due to financial constraints, both girls had to leave school before completing Form 4. According to the local customs, she went through initiation and married her husband Limbani at the age of 16. He works as a fisherman, she works in the garden, but as she started having children immediately, the opportunities open to her are limited. She respects the cultural norm that requires abstaining from sex during the first weeks after delivery. Her husband is not willing to abstain; he believes that a real man has to perform. Financially he is not stable enough to marry another wife; therefore, he meets his girlfriend every now and then.*

If we analyse this case study, we see that the behaviour of both and the role they perform in society is determined by biological factors on one hand and social and cultural factors on the other. The fact the

Pilira has given birth and that her husband impregnates her are consequences of their biological making. The decision of Pilira's family to allow the boys to continue with their education, to send the children to undergo initiation and her decision to follow the custom to abstain are consequences of her culture and the society she lives in.

When we refer to the roles, expectations, responsibilities, and attitudes that society creates for males and females, we talk about **gender**. Although it is usually linked to the **sex** of a person, it is not the same thing. Sex is determined by our biology – we are either male or female – while gender is created by society. As a result, gender roles and sex roles are also different.

Gender	Sex
• Is created by the society or community we live in. • Depends on our culture and traditions. • It is learned behaviour – for example, women are not 'born to cook' – some cultures and societies just expect them to while in others, it is the men who cook.	• Is biological - you are either male or female. • It is universal – you will be a man or a woman wherever you are, regardless of the culture or the society you live in. • Your sex cannot be changed (except by surgery).

Gender roles	Sex roles

• Gender roles change over time. For example, in the past, women could not vote because the political role in society was reserved for men. Now, women in an increasing number of countries all over the world have been	• Are the roles that males and females have in sex and reproduction.
	• Sex roles include:
	  ○ Women's role to give birth.
	  ○ Women's role to breast feed.

enfranchised.
• They vary within the same society between social classes, age groups, urban and rural areas etc. For example, the behaviour of older rural women differs significantly from that of similar aged urban women.
• Gender roles include:
   o Women's role to cook, nurse the sick and care for children.
   o Men's role to look after their families, make decisions and be in charge.
	o Men's role to impregnate women.

Adapted from: Lekani Nkhanza Training Manual, Zomba 2005

So, men and women perform different roles due to their biological differences – women bear children, men impregnate women – as a consequence of their biological make-up. Socialisation however is a process that we go through – from the moment we are born, to the moment we die. It is the way that we are shaped as males and females by our families, neighbours and the community we live in – and by our customs, beliefs and even the laws of the country.

Almost everything in our lives influences the way we act and the roles we play. This includes:
- Our history
- What we learn from parents, teachers, friends, religious leaders, and traditional leaders and healers
- The community we live in
- The schools and churches we go to
- The chores we are given as children
- Our cultural practices

This happens over our whole lives, from birth to death.

Adapted from: Lekani Nkhanza Manual, Zomba 2005

During the socialisation process:
- Different manners for males and females get established and cemented.
- Attitudes of males and females towards each other are formed.
- The personalities of males and females are created and established.
- Power and values are determined for males and females.
- The relationship of subordination and domination between females and males is established and reinforced.

Society and culture start to influence the behaviour, roles and responsibilities of male and female children from the moment they are born. For example, to send out a message that a male child is born, women prolong their ululation while for a female child, the ululation is very brief. This sends a message that a boy is more important than a girl.

When it comes to household chores, boys are taught not to do caregiving work like washing dishes, learning how to cook or taking care of smaller siblings.

Even the toys parents give their children send messages. Boys are given masculine toys like cars, aeroplanes, bows, arrows and guns. These symbolize strength and the roles and responsibilities they might have in future. For girls, toys include dolls or toy pots and other cooking utensils. These show the care giving role the girl will be expected to perform in future.

When parents with little money are forced to decide which of their children they will send to school, most choose to send the boys.

So, our behaviour is a consequence of our biological make-up and of the socialization process we go through during our whole life. But what are the consequences of the different roles? Can they be linked to the spread of *nkhanza*?

In most societies, more value is attached to the tasks performed by men while female work is not highly valued. Paid jobs are considered more important for the maintenance of the family than the work done by women. Women's family-rearing and subsistence farming roles are not regarded as real work because they don't bring money into the home.

In practice, the amount of work done by the average women is far greater and more important for survival than that done by the average man. Yet most of a woman's contribution might be hard to see because:
- Women are more likely to be found working without pay at home and in producing food, while most jobs with salaries are held by men.
- Work done by women is physical, intensive, and time consuming. They therefore work longer hours and with less rest.
- Women are likely to be involved in a number of roles at the same time. They may be busy, bringing up a family and doing community work (like helping with funerals, weddings and religious events) all at the same time

The problem is not that men and women perform different roles, but the resulting distribution of power and influence that usually favours men and makes women vulnerable to many forms of *nkhanza*.

Acts of *nkhanza* (like economic abuse) are also linked to the way men see themselves as the sole breadwinner. They see the money they earn as belonging to them alone – even though their partner may have contributed her labour or made it possible for her husband to go and work without having to worry about raising the children.

The above is a brief discussion on the different roles men and women perform in marriage and society as are a consequence of their biological make-up and mainly because of their socialization and culture. We have also seen that the fact that men and women perform different roles is not generally problematic, but *nkhanza* occurs when different values are added to the specific roles, such that one sex believes it is superior to the other.

So, the panellists will discuss now how the roles should be distributed within a marriage to avoid *nkhanza*:

Fac: We would like to ask you to clarify the roles that should be played by the husband and by the wife respectively within a marriage.

Law: As we know there are different responsibilities in marriage. For example, looking after the household, taking care of the children and working so that the family has an income. Maybe the Sheikh can add on what other responsibilities there are, particularly here in the village.

Sheikh: As it has been explained, there are different types of responsibilities in marriage here in the village as everyone knows. There are responsibilities, which both parties can partake in like sweeping the house and other duties.

T/A: It is true that in our tradition there are duties that a man and woman or husband and wife can both take part in but there are some responsibilities that are fit only for a man as tradition stipulates, same applies to a woman.

Fac: Let us say the whole family, father, mother and children have gone to the farm to till the land. Upon their return, the meal has to be prepared, served and of course eaten. Amongst these duties, are there some responsibilities that can bring about abuse?

T/A: As I said before that amongst the responsibilities that are in a marriage, there are some responsibilities that are solely for the man and some for the woman. If the married couple goes together and works in their farm, when they set off to go home, the man can get a log for fire wood which he will cut when they get home, Meanwhile the wife collects the hoes and looks for some okra for relish. These are the duties that a married couple can assist each other with. Further more, when they get home, whilst the mother is busy with the household chores, if there is a child, the father may assist by looking after and playing with the child, whilst the mother is busy preparing the meal.

Sheikh: God tells us in the Qur'an that: "you should live harmoniously with your wife". He also says: "men are the leaders". You will find a leader in most situations. Usually when there is no leader, there is no progress or harmony. That is why God shows us in his Holy Book that "men are the leaders", but this does not mean that you should leave all the duties to the weaker one, even those that the woman will not be able to carry out. Being a leader means making sure that he will take up all the major responsibilities as the head of the family and make sure that he carries them out accordingly. He should not take advantage of his wife leaving her responsibilities that she is incapable of since he is the head of the family.

In the Qur'an you will find things that God explained a long time ago. God explained that there is no difference between people. Everyone is equal, except on things that either sex is unable to do; those will be done by the capable sex only. For example, breast-feeding, this is a woman's duty. It is impossible for a man to breast-feed since he does not have breasts. Therefore, those duties that a man cannot perform should be left for a woman and vice versa.

Law: The law says that everyone has human rights as mentioned in the Constitution or in the Universal Declaration of Human Rights. The main point that arises from having human rights is that sexual discrimination should not be practised when applying responsibilities in a family. We should all work as Malawian citizens.

As the Sheikh explained, there are certain things that can only be done by a particular sex due to biological make up like breast-feeding or child bearing. Such things cannot be changed. These are a woman's responsibilities. There are also some responsibilities that are fit for a particular sex due to tradition. We have all seen both men and women working in the field, which means that both men and women can perform this task. Another thing that can be done by both the husband and wife is looking after of the home. The law says we have the freedom to perform these duties regardless of whether one is a man, woman, boy or girl. That is how I can put it in short.

Fac: What should happen in the following situation when the family returns from the fields? The mother is pregnant and there is an infant as well. Is it proper that she carries the hoes on her head, the infant on her back; furthermore, upon arrival at home, she should search for firewood and start preparing the meal, because she is a woman? While, all this is being done the husband sits and waits for bathing water and for his meal, is this proper?

T/A: As we have said before, assisting each other is part of our tradition putting aside those activities that men cannot take part in. To answer your question, when this family returns from the fields, if they have an infant and the mother is expectant, it is the husband's duty to carry the infant in order to help the mother. That is what our culture teaches us. We found our elders doing this, helping with carrying or playing with the child in order to assist the mother.

Upon arrival at home, if the wife is unable to cook, and you as the husband can see that she is tired, you will have to assist with the household chores such as cooking. In the days of our elders, families had a tradition of helping one another in such circumstances.

Sheikh: A man and wife should live peacefully in a marriage. They should help each other in the various duties that are expected of them. There is nowhere in the Qur'an where specific duties are assigned to a particular sex. For example, the cooking of *nsima* is not assigned to the woman only or to the man. It is emphasised that both men and woman are capable of carrying out household duties. A man, for example, can wash clothes just as well as a woman. In fact he is stronger than a woman. The same applies to the cooking of *nsima*. There are however some duties that are traditionally carried out by men as explained to us by the T/A, building of a house for example. These traditions cannot be changed due to the fact that a woman is weaker, there are some things that she is be able to do and therefore such things should be left for the men to carry out.

The Qur'an further goes on to tell us about employment. It says that a woman can be employed as long as she follows the Islamic laws. There is no law against woman finding employment. God says also in the Holy Qur'an that the man has the responsibility of looking after his wife's needs. This does not mean that if the wife is employed, she is therefore equal to the man. It means the money the woman earns, whether she is employed or she is operating a business, belongs to the woman. She is not expected to look after the family with her earnings. It further indicates that the man, since he was given the responsibility of looking after his wife and children, is therefore responsible for the family's financial needs. This however does not mean that the wife's earnings can not be used in the household. She can, of her own accord, contribute to the family's income as they live together harmoniously as a family.

Fac: We will now ask our lawyer to conclude and thereafter we will take some questions.

Law: In the law, the point that is emphasized is that there is to be no discrimination between a woman and a man or a boy and a girl when daily duties are being carried out. As we have said before, there are indeed some functions, as we all know, that can only be carried out by a particular sex due to our biological make up, such as giving birth and breast-feeding. The other duties, as we have heard from the Sheikh and our Traditional Authority, are jobs that can be done by both the man and the woman together.

Fac: Now, if there are any questions, please go ahead and ask. The panel here will respond to your questions.

Question: I have a question from what I have heard, I believe that men and women assist each other with their daily duties but is it acceptable for the wife to say that she has been cooking *nsima* for the past two days and she is tired so it is now the husband's turn to cook, and if he does not cook, he will not eat?

T/A: Thank you very much. In our tradition, it is not proper for the wife to say she has been cooking for the past two days and therefore it is now the husband's turn. Traditionally, this is not acceptable. It is a sign of abuse since one party is forcing the other because when one assists the other, it is to be done willingly.

On the other hand, we are not saying that the man cannot cook *nsima* to help his wife, but, the man may one day retaliate by saying that he has been buying relish for the past two days and therefore it is now the wife's turn when the wife is incapable of providing the family with relish or clothing for that matter. The man should, however, be in a position to assist his wife in a situation whereby he can see that she is tired or when she has a lot of chores to deal with. We have also observed that usually men do assist with the cooking but what stops them from doing so is some of the women's attitude of publicising the fact that her husband has been cooking *nsima* in their household and therefore he is now weak. Some men then get discouraged due to the women not being able to keep their mouths shut. Instead of being proud of the fact that her husband assists her, she goes about disgracing her husband. In turn the husband feels humiliated.

Sheikh: The most important things in a marriage are love and respect. We say that a couple should assist one another, we are not saying one party is inferior to the other but that there should be mutual love and respect between the two. The response made by the woman that, "I have been cooking for the past few days", shows that there is lack of love between the two. In the end, the marriage is destroyed. Therefore, there should be mutual respect between the two as it should always be because Islam promotes this culture as well.

Conclusion

From the above it is clear that the roles and tasks attributed to men and women in marriage differ slightly, but the three panellists agree that this should not lead to any form of discrimination against one spouse.

Islam and tradition consider the man as the leader of the household; he should be responsible for the maintenance, protection, and overall leadership of the family, within the framework of consultation and kindness. The law does not make any statement regarding the different tasks of men and women in marriage.

All three panellists agree that mutual respect should be the guiding principle when decisions are taken regarding the distribution of tasks within the household. If one is tired or sick, the other should take over. Supporting, considering and respecting each other is seen as the key to a peaceful and harmonious marriage, something that all couples should achieve.

Expectations and consequences of a marriage

"Marriage is perseverance" – "Banja ndikupilira" (Malawian proverb)

"And among His signs is this, that He created for you mates from among yourselves, that you may dwell in peace and tranquillity with them, and He has put love and mercy between your (hearts): Verily in that are signs for those who reflect" (Qur'an, 30:21).

"The family is the natural and fundamental group unit of society and is entitled to protection by society and the State." (Malawi Constitution 22,1)

A lot of *nkhanza* takes place in the home, between people married to each other, their children and their families. Part of the reason for this seems to be the way people see marriage and their understanding of what marriage means.

The romantic idea of marriage is that people get married because they love each other and want to start a family. As a result, one would expect that marriages are caring relationships with neither party ever wanting to harm the other.

In reality though, many people have little or no choice about who to marry, when to marry or even whether to marry or not. Instead, they get married because their culture demands it or because their family and community expect them to be married and have children.

Research by WLSA Malawi, for example, found that in the Nkhota-kota district (where polygamy is practiced), there is great cultural pressure on men to have more than one wife. If they don't they are accused of 'hiding something'.

Arranged marriages are also quite common in some communities. Parents may arrange to marry off their children so that two families will be connected, so that they don't have to keep providing for their daughters or to get closer to the other family's wealth.

Social and economic factors also play a role. Some people marry for more property, more money or to avoid terrible poverty. This is especially true for women who are usually less economically empowered than men.

Poverty is also responsible for 'temporary' or 'seasonal' marriages, which come about because many jobs are seasonal.

As a result, many marriages have nothing to do with love. Instead, people find themselves married to people they may not know very well or even like. This may affect what people expect of their spouse within a marriage. Because they spend so much time together and face all of life's problems together, tensions inevitably arise that often lead to conflict and *nkhanza*.

But even if the couple married because they love each other and both of them plan to live together happily; differing expectations about what marriage means may lead to *nkhanza*.
- Some people believe that customary practices (like 'educational beatings') are a part of being married.
- Most societies expect women to endure everything that happens.
- Some people believe they are automatically entitled to all the property that the other spouse owned before the marriage.

But, those are not necessarily consequences of a marriage, because marriage and its consequences are covered by the law, either customary or statutory. For religious people, the rules and commandments of their leaders might be another guiding principle. As a result we need to look at what the representatives of Islam, the Traditional Authority and Law say about what it means to be married and what somebody who intends to marry – or is already married – can expect from his or her spouse:

Fac: We are here today to discuss the expectations of marriage. If we are not aware of what expectations there are in a marriage, this could be the basis of abuse. We should also know what the consequences are of the type of marriage we enter. If we don't know what the laws are that govern that particular marriage, we might accept an abusive relationship without knowing how to defend ourselves. I will therefore ask my colleagues what types of marriages there are in Malawi.

Law: If we look at Section 22 of the Constitution of Malawi, freedom is given to all to marry. In this same section, the types of marriages that are legally acceptable are also outlined. There is the marriage that is registered with the Registrar General where a marriage certificate is obtained. The second type is a traditional ceremony. The third type of a marriage is one that can be done in accordance with Islam or any other Religion. The fourth is the one whereby a couple may cohabit. The laws of this country take these four types as legal marriages.

Fac: So out of these four legal marriages, what types of marriage are the most common ones here in Mangochi?

T/A: Here in Mangochi, the most common type of marriage is when a man has proposed to a woman and the woman has accepted. The man then finds out from the woman who her a*nkhoswe* (mediator) is so that an *nkhoswe* from his side can meet him and ask for her hand in marriage. The two sides then meet and discuss and ask the woman if she has accepted the proposal. The couple is not expected to cohabit before being married. Only after agreeing, can they start making wedding arrangements in accordance with the Islamic Religion. The discussions include all aspects of the celebrations like the acceptance of gifts by the bride and groom and the blessing done by the Sheikh, which makes the marriage official.

Another type of marriage that we have here is when the couple cohabits. This kind of a marriage is not generally accepted, because when problems arise, neither the woman's nor the man's side recognise the marriage. So they don't have anyone who can assist them if they have problems. This may lead to "divorce" since the two may not be able to solve the problem on their own. In this type of union, problems may also arise when children are involved.

Fac: Now we would like to ask the lawyer if she has ever heard of people who live together for a long time and when the woman asks them to get married officially, the man refuses. Does this happen and if it does what would you advise women to do in such a situation?

Law: Indeed, this is very common. Men do this so that when there is trouble in the marriage, the woman does not have any where to go and report. But our Constitution clearly states in section 22 that arrangements where there is no official agreement or *ankhoswe,* are for all intents and purposes legal marriages. All people who are cohabiting as husband and wife have the same rights as those whose marriages have been formalised and the matter can be brought to court for resolution.

Fac: Taking into consideration the types of marriages mentioned by the T/A, what can a man expect from his wife or a woman from her husband when he or she enters marriage?

Sheikh: When the marriage has been finalized, the wife expects to live peacefully with her husband. The Qur'an tells us that the man is supposed to live with his wife peacefully without any abuse whatsoever. The woman also expects the man to provide for her financially. He should clothe her, provide food and so forth.

Fac: Does this mean that if the man does not cloth or feed her, he is not meeting her expectations?

Sheikh: According to Islam, that means the man is not meeting his wife's expectations. But this does not mean that if the man is poor or struggling to make ends meet, the woman should force him to provide for her to the extent of pressurising him. The man should provide for her in accordance with his capabilities. The fact is the man is responsible for looking after his wife regardless of his financial status. The wife also expects to be treated well by her husband, not to be treated like a domestic animal, this means without any physical abuse. The Islamic Religion does not permit that.

In turn, the woman is supposed to safeguard her husband's wealth. I'm emphasising this because there are some women who spend their husband's wealth lavishly, without a second thought, just because they do not have to earn or work for it.

Another point is that in accordance with Islam, the wife should not leave the house without the husband's permission.

Fac: Please clarify this, is the woman supposed to ask for permission to leave the house at all times? Is it permissible for a man to go anywhere he wants at any time without asking for permission from his wife?

Sheikh: In short we can say asking for permission applies to both parties but it is mainly directed to the woman because the man is the head of the family. If the man wants to go somewhere, he should notify his wife of where he is going, irrespective of the fact that he is the head of the household. In case anything happens, the woman should be able to know where her husband is.

Fac: Is it permitted for a husband to have many wives?

T/A: According to our Yao culture, a man can have more than one wife.
Law: Within the marriages that I mentioned earlier, only the traditional one allows the man to have more than one wife on condition that he has permission from the first wife. In order to have more than one wife, the man has to follow certain procedures: the new woman is supposed to be known to both families and the community as a wife so in order to differentiate between polygamy and extra-marital affairs.

Marriages conducted at the Registrar General's office, do not allow polygamy.

Fac: In our culture, what if a man marries two or three wives after being married to just one, is this not abuse?

Law: The laws that govern traditional marriage allow a man to have more than one wife. So if a man gets another wife or wives, this is not abuse. Abuse may start as a result of how the man went about getting the other wife or wives. He is supposed to get the consent of the first wife or other wives before taking a new one.

T/A: Taking a second wife is not abuse in accordance with the Yao culture and Islamic Religion. Islam permits a man to have more than one wife, he is allowed up to four wives as mentioned in the Qur'an. Since the women in this area are Muslims, when their husbands marry a second or third wife, they do not see anything wrong with that since it is permitted by our religion. It is considered *nkhanza* when a man has three wives, for example, and he only looks after one or two and neglects the other by not going to her house, not building a house for her or not providing clothing.

Fac: In the matter of sexual relations, how can abuse be avoided?

T/A: A good marriage is based on two people trusting and respecting each other as well as following the guidelines that are found in a marriage. Between the two people, one day the man may be tired or vice versa. In such circumstances, they should respect each other and not use force. If they do so, that will be *nkhanza*.

Sheikh: God has said in the Qur'an that the purpose of a marriage is for a husband or wife to live peacefully without any anxiety. According to the question, the T/A has already told us how it is supposed to be. It does not differ from what the Qur'an says. The only thing is that the "tiredness" should not become a habit but instead the couple can just postpone to another suitable time.

Fac: The important lesson that we should get here is that there should not be forced sex in a marriage and neither should one partner deliberately deny the other.

Question: From what I heard from the lady concerning officiating of a marriage, I would like to know what I as a woman can do to make the man make the marriage official?

Law: If you live with a man and you are happy and yet the man refuses to make it official, the law still recognizes you as a married couple. The Constitution says if a man and a woman live together like an officially married couple, in the same house for years, they are recognized as a married couple

Question: I would like to know from the sheikh what steps are being taken to prevent the spread of AIDS when people want to practise polygamy?

Sheikh: Because of the way we live nowadays, a man cannot just go out and get another wife without following certain procedures since there is a deadly disease in our midst. There are centres that are available where one can have a blood test done. If the man wants to practise polygamy, he and his intended bride should both go for blood tests. If the blood test shows that they are in good health, then they can proceed with the marriage. This should be done every time the man wants a new wife.

Conclusion

As we have seen, each institution expects married people to behave in a particular way; certain rights are given to the spouses within a marriage, but also obligations. Where a partner fails to fulfil their obligations, the other is able to ask for a divorce.[5]

During the last dialogue we have already learned that according to Islam, Tradition and Malawian law, both partners have the right to live with each other and enjoy each other's company. The husband has the obligation to provide a house for his wife or wives and he is responsible for feeding his wife or wives and their children. The wife, on the other hand is responsible for taking care of the household and the children.

Polygamy is allowed by customary law, Islam and Constitution, provided that certain rules are followed. Contrary to Islam, that allows a man to marry a maximum of four wives, Constitutional and customary law do not limit the number of wives, provided – and here there is agreement with Islam – that he can afford to look after or maintain all of them. Other conditions for entering a polygamous marriage are:

- Before a man can marry another wife, the consent of the first wife or the other wives must be sought.
- Each wife must be housed and must be provided with a garden to work in.
- The husband must devote equal lengths of time and love to each wife.
- The first wife has seniority over all the other wives and it is usually her children who inherit any chieftaincy.
- Each wife has access to property used in her household.
- The husband is not allowed to have adulterous affairs. If he wants another woman, he must first marry her after seeking consent from the first wife or wives.

Another point that was high lightened was the importance of satisfactory sexual relations within the marriage. This implies that neither men nor women have the right to deny the other sex without good reason for any length of time. An acceptable reason might be the birth of a child, menstruation or tiredness after working too much.

---

[5] No institution regards divorce as the preferable way out of a difficult situation; they all have different means and ways of promoting a reconciliation. These as well as divorce will be discussed in a later chapter.

An important prerequisite for a marriage to be valid is the consent of the involved parties. According to the panellists, without the necessary consent of the spouses, the ankhoswe and sometimes the parents, a marriage is not considered a legally binding marriage contract; the couple might face problems afterwards. The agreed procedure is that the groom proposes and the bride accepts, afterwards the ankhoswe have to agree.

To summarise, according to Islamic and traditional principles as well as to Malawian law, during a marriage each spouse can expect the fulfilment of the following conditions because they are considered fundamental principles of a marriage:

1. The husband and wife have the right to live with each other as husband and wife and enjoy each other's company.
2. For as long as they are married, a husband and wife have a **reasonable right** to sexual intercourse with each other. This does not mean however that a husband can demand sex whenever he wants. Every institution allows women to refuse sex during menstruation, after surgery, immediately after childbirth, or in any similar situation.
3. The husband will not take additional wives without the consent of the other wife or wives.
4. The couple must respect each other's rights and will not assault each other.
5. The husband will provide a house for his wife or wives.
6. The husband will support his wife or wives and children by providing for their needs.
7. The wife will take care of the household and generally take care of the children.

So we can observe that a lot of practices, that take place in some families, are contrary to these principles and are violating Islamic principles as well as traditional and statutory law. Some of them are:

1. Husband or wife beating, either correctional or any other beating.
2. Withholding food or other necessities from a wife to punish her.
3. Locking the husband or wife out if they come home late.

4. Having extra-marital affairs.
5. That a husband will automatically own the property of his wife.
6. That a wife will automatically own the property of her husband.
7. Property grabbing
8. Unreasonably forcing a partner to have sex when they don't want to.
9. Having unprotected sex with your partner even though you know you are infected with HIV.
10. Not allowing a partner to seek medical attention for HIV/AIDS or any other sexually transmitted disease just because you don't want people to know that you are both sick.
11. That everything that happens in the home has to be kept secret.
12. That a husband or wife must give up their religion and take up the religion of the other.
13. Any other kind of cruelty or *nkhanza*.
14. Any other crime.

Adapted from: Lekani Nkhanza Training Manual, 2005

All three institutions agree that the above mentioned practices are at the very least legitimate grounds for divorce (in particular extra-marital affairs or desertion). Other practices are considered a crime by the law and can be punished through imprisonment (beating the spouse, property grabbing). The above mentioned issues will be covered in the following chapters.

Extra-marital affairs

"Women are like relish, you need to have a lot" – "Mkazi ali ngati ndiwo anafuna kumasintha" (Malawian proverb)

"Nor come near to adultery, for it is an indecent (deed) and evil way (Qur'an 17:32)

"A petition for divorce may be presented to the Court either by the husband or wife on the ground that the respondent has since the celebration of the marriage committed adultery. " (Section 5 of the Divorce Act)

Extra-marital affairs are not acceptable. All over the world we hear a similar statement when different people are asked about extra-marital affairs. Adultery is considered morally reprehensible, as it threatens to break up the family, and endangers the health of the spouse and maybe the whole family, just to mention a few reasons.

But although it is condemned, adultery happens everywhere, all the time and in all cultures, not only in Malawi. *"It happens a lot here, we all do it, but many do not know that it is bad, they just do it. But we all know that there is Aids around. We have lots of fights about it in our households but woman have no rights anyway, and can not ask for a divorce."* (Woman from Mangochi District)

But while public opinion condemns extra-marital affairs, some people seem to encourage it. Which male reader has never heard men at a drinking place showing off about the number of girlfriends they have? Which faithful husband has not been ridiculed by his peer-group when defending his decision to stay faithful to his wife? The author recalls vividly what happened during an HIV/Aids awareness training course; the Facilitator asked those men to raise their hands, who during the last five years had gone to a training course or workshop and had never committed adultery. Not a single hand was held up. Was this because all men committed adultery or because the ones who were faithful where ashamed of it?

So it seems that it is part of the male role in society to have as many girlfriends as possible. The ones, who have a lot of girlfriends are considered "real or wealthy men", while the others are believed to be not very virile or simply poor. *"We try to abstain but it must be a force from Satan?"* (Man from Mangochi). Therefore, when men engage in extra-marital affairs, their spouses are supposed to forgive them. But if a woman does the same, it is at least a reason for immediate divorce, in the worst case the husband can beat her to death.

Contrary to male peer-groups, female peer-groups don't encourage adultery; maybe because it is not linked to femininity. Older women usually advise younger wives, who complain that their husbands are having affairs, to persevere and to consider it as a normal male behaviour. Only recently it has been reported that younger women recommend their fellow women, who are being betrayed, to also betray their husbands as a form of vengeance. *"Sometimes it is like a race: who cheats first".*

To summarise, it seems that a lot of men and some women like to cheat on their partners, but it becomes evident, that nobody wants to be betrayed. Being betrayed by one's partner is considered by **everybody** as a severe form of *nkhanza*. Our panelists are going to discuss the different reasons for and consequences of extra-marital affairs.

Fac: In our discussions today, we would like to find out how abuse comes about when one spouse has an extra-marital affair. First we would like to ask the T/A to clarify what an extra-marital affair is.

T/A: An extra-marital affair is when a married person has another or several other relationships outside the marriage.

Fac: We would like to hear from the religious and legal points of view if this is allowed.

Sheikh: Extra-marital affairs are bad and no one in a marriage is permitted to have an affair. It is not permitted in Islam.

Law: In agreement with the Sheikh, the law does not permit extra-marital affairs. The law does not permit a married man or woman to have a sexual relationship with another person outside of marriage.

T/A: Extra- marital affairs are not permitted in a marriage. But in our culture we have the *mdulo* concept. For example: When a man had an extra-marital affair during his wife's pregnancy, this could result in the death of the unborn child. In this case it was taboo for him to go back to his wife and continue having sexual relationship with her since the household was considered tainted. The elders first had to meet and choose a man to go and sleep with the wife as a way of cleansing the household. In those days, that was the tradition and so it was normal but that does not apply today. It was considered as an act of cleansing, not as an extra-marital affair or adultery.

Fac: So now we see that it was not a promiscuous act but it was permitted by tradition in the event of a child dying in the family when the husband had had an affair. Why then do we say extra-marital affairs are a form of *nkhanza*? What happens? What are the results?

Sheikh: Faithfulness in a marriage is required for several very important reasons. It is how parentage can be confirmed. If a man is unfaithful, he may have a child somewhere who will not know its father. If a woman is unfaithful, the father of the child will not be known. It is only those who are married that have a right to sexual intercourse with each other.

So faithfulness is extremely important to parenthood, but also to protect the lives of the two people. If they are faithful they will have healthy and productive lives but if they are not, the risk of getting sexually transmitted diseases such as AIDS is very high. This may result in death which in turn will affect the children who may be orphaned.

T/A: There are a lot of different problems that can make a family discordant when one partner has an extra-marital affair. Firstly: the one who has an extra-marital affair may contract a sexually transmitted disease and then pass it on to his or her partner.

Secondly: there is a lack of trust between the couple because one is going behind the others back and having an affair. The results, as we all know are: if one contracts AIDS and passes it on to the partner, the chances that both of them die and leave orphans, is very high. This then causes problems for the orphaned children since they will have no one to look after them, pay for their education and provide the other essential things that children need to grow as God intended.

Another form of *nkhanza* is when the innocent party gets depressed and as a consequence there is no harmony in the family.

If it is the husband having an affair, the family usually is not well looked after in terms of food and clothing just to mention a few essentials. This not only affects the wife but the children as well because the husband is unlikely to go to his "girlfriend" empty handed. He therefore deprives the family whilst spending lavishly on the "girlfriend."

Fac: Let's see how a man whose wife is having an extra-marital affair is affected, how does he feel when is amongst his friends?

Law: As we saw in our play, the man whose wife is having an affair feels offended. He falls into a deep depression. In addition to this, we see that his wife does not respect him as the head of the household. So, the wife and her boyfriend take away any dignity he has. This is another form of abuse that affects the husband..

Fac: Now we would like to see why do spouses get involved in these affairs, knowing the negative impacts mentioned?

Sheikh: One reason for extra-marital affairs is that one spouse is not satisfied sexually with the other. Another might be that there is lack of trust between the two that leads to a lack of love, which then further leads the spouses to indulge in extra-marital affairs. Another reason may be because the husband is not looking after his family properly. When he has money and does not provide for his wife and children as well as God says he should, this may leave the wife desperate and thereby leading her to get involved with another man.

For a husband to get involved in an extra-marital affair, it may be due to the fact that his wife is sick or because the couple has failed to produce any children together. Therefore the man decides to try elsewhere.

Fac: As a Tradional Authority, do you think these reasons make extra-marital affairs acceptable?

T/A: The issue of extra-marital affairs in a marriage is wrong. The reasons that may lead to extra-marital affairs, although they are wrong, are many. At times, the husband gets involved in an extra-marital affair because the wife is not kind, is selfish, or denies him any sexual contact.

At times extra-marital affairs may arise if the man fails to satisfy his wife sexually, sometimes intentionally, sometimes due to physical reasons. Due to her sexual needs, she may resort to having an extra-marital affair. But if the problem is that the man cannot sexually satisfy his wife then there are traditional herbal remedies that may be used. There is no need for the wife to go and have an extra-marital affair, all the man has to do is to take the herbs orally and these will be able to give him the strength that he needs. These herbs may also be used in the case of impotence.

In order to solve their problems, the couple should sit down and discuss the issue at hand. If one party still feels disgruntled, then they may have to separate or divorce instead of getting involved in extra-marital affairs.

Fac: Let us see what the Malawian Law says on this topic. What should be done when there has been an extra-marital affair in a marriage?

Law: The law that governs this country, the Constitution explains that the family is the natural and fundamental group unit of society. This means that people should respect the marriage bond. When a man and a woman enter marriage, they are announcing to everybody that they have entered into a contract with each other. If any of the two had any other relationships prior to the marriage or if during the engagement one of the spouses meets someone else who he or she is attracted to, the moment they enter into the marriage contact, they vow that they will not get involved with anyone else. As a consequence, when a spouse gets involved in an extra-marital affair, he or she does not respect his or her partner and they may also lose their self-respect.

It also means that if a person feels he cannot be sexually satisfied with one wife, the Malawian Law allows for that man to have more than one wife, but not if the marriage is conducted at the Registrar General's office.

Fac: We now know that extra-marital affairs are neither permitted by religion nor by tradition; having an extra-marital affair is a form of *nkhanza*. Now the panel will take your questions.

Question: I would like to ask the Traditional Authority about the traditional remedies you talked about earlier. Are the remedies given to the man or to the woman? Are these remedies available these days because a lot of marriages are ending because of partners not being sexually fulfilled in a marriage? If they are available, please make them accessible to all that are in need so that those marriages may have their problem solved.

T/A: The traditional remedies I talked about earlier which help restore sexual drive and cure impotence were available in the days of our ancestors and are still available today. The plants and herbs are still available in our forests even if they have been mismanaged by the community. There are traditional healers who have the remedies on hand. These remedies can restore ones sexual drive and may cure impotence.

Question: Honourable Sheikh, in our culture, we allow a man to have more than four wives, but we still find problems in the homes. People are using this as an excuse to have extra-marital affairs, so what are the proper channels that one should follow when practising legalised polygamy?

Sheikh: To be honest in the Islamic Religion, polygamy is what is curbing extra-marital affairs. The réasons being: When a man has one wife, we all know that it is not possible for him to have sexual relations with his wife every single day of the month due to a woman's biological makeup, i.e. menstrual cycle. It is also known that when a woman gives birth, she is supposed to abstain from sexual intercourse for four months or more. As a man of sound health, would you be able to abstain for that long?

Now in Islam, to avoid extra-marital affairs, polygamy is permitted so that when a woman is supposed to abstain, the man will not have to wait for the woman. If he can not, he might have an extra-marital affair and come back with a sexually transmitted disease that infects his wife.

Question: I have a question concerning abuse. This particularly concerns women. When a woman is found guilty of committing adultery, the husband has the right to end the marriage automatically, without any discussions taking place. But if the man is the one who is guilty, usually discussions take place. Is this not abuse?

T/A: What we can say is, between the two people, the one who has committed adultery can apologize to the innocent party but if the innocent person does not forgive his or her partner, then divorce may be granted.

Sheikh: The Holy Qur'an tells us that if one of the two is in the wrong, regardless if it is the man or the woman then their mediators are supposed to meet and discuss the situation amicably.

Question: My question is directed to our lawyer. The main issue nowadays is AIDS. I understand that the law says, if someone commits murder, he or she should stand trial and be executed if found guilty. If a man, for example, dies of AIDS, another man may get involved with the widow. Now when the new husband contracts the disease and dies, how would you as a lawyer, prosecute the woman?

Law: This country has passed a law called: *"National Policy on HIV/AIDS"*. Since everyone has a right to marry, we marry by choice and follow the guidelines outlined by our culture and by the Islamic Religion. There is no law that states that a person should be tested for HIV/AIDS before they enter marriage but in my opinion a law should be put in place to that effect.

As stated in the question, when the man dies, perhaps due to the fact that the woman has infected him, the problem is that it is difficult to prove that it is this particular woman who has indeed infected him. The law in fact says that one who causes loss of life should in turn loose his or her life, but this law depends on the availability of solid proof. For example: Someone kills another person with an axe. When the case goes to court, the axe is used as evidence and if there were eye witnesses available they are also called to tell the court what they saw.

In this particular instance, if both partners were not tested before they got married, it is difficult to prove that the second husband has died due to the fact that that the woman in question infected him.

Since there is no law that demands that couples should be tested before they enter marriage, we as individuals have the obligation to protect ourselves. We can get tested before we enter marriage. We can go to a hospital and get tested. There are a lot of hospitals that are equipped to conduct HIV/AIDS tests, for example government hospitals or private institutions such as Macro.

You might want to avoid getting tested and confront the woman directly and ask her if her husband died of AIDS. Probably the answer she will give you is that her husband did not die of AIDS but he had Tuberculosis or she might not know the real reason behind his death.

Question: I work in South Africa. When I left Malawi, my wife was pregnant. She gave birth whilst I was at work. I sent money and other things to support my wife and child. Upon my return, I find that she is pregnant with another man's child. A man I do not know. Should I go back to the marriage or should I leave this woman?

Law: In the eyes of the law, one of the grounds for divorce is if there is proof of infidelity. The man in such a case has the right to go to court and file for divorce and demand an apology from the woman because she will have wronged her husband. So in answer to your question that you come from South Africa and find your wife pregnant, that is enough proof that she committed adultery when you were away and so you can get a divorce and get re-married to someone who will be faithful to you.

Sheikh: In addition, even in Islam, a woman caught committing adultery is acceptable grounds for divorce. If she is pregnant it is an irrefutable proof that she cannot deny because she can not just get pregnant without having committed adultery. So a divorce will be granted but you should go to the chief or to court where a divorce can be granted.

Fac: The question asked by the gentleman was if in such a situation, he should go back or not?

Law: As I mentioned before, these are grounds for divorce but there is no law which forces the man to divorce his wife because the woman has committed adultery. In Christianity it is said if you cannot forgive the one who has wronged you, you may divorce but it is up to you if you want to forgive her or not. So if you want to forgive her and stay together and resume your life, it is all up to you.

Sheikh: When we look at the question that was put before us, we see that it is not prohibited if a person wants to go back to his wife. We can not stop him because the right to marry or not is that of an individual. Religion cannot dictate that just because of what has happened that there must be a separation. Maybe that person is fine with what happened, we do not know. Maybe he will go back because he was doing the same thing when he was away so he does not see why his wife could not do the same. All religions say that adultery is a valid enough reason for a couple to get a divorce. The choice is yours to either divorce or stay married.

Conclusion

Neither Islam, nor Tradition nor Malawian law, accept adultery, they all consider it morally reprehensible.. Extramarital sex on one hand is a **type of** *nkhanza* itself as it humiliates the betrayed partner. On the other hand, it might be also a **cause of** more *nkhanza* in the family. For example, violence often results when a person finds out that their partner has been having sex with someone else. Economic abuse happens when a spouse spends all of the family's money on their lover.

The panellists agreed further, that possible consequences of adultery may be:
- The complete breakdown of the marriage.
- The risk of HIV infection. The more sexual partners one has, the greater the chance of getting infected and then infecting your spouse.
- The risk of other sexually transmitted diseases (like gonorrhoea and syphilis). These can damage the reproductive organs and cause infertility and even death.
- Economic hardship because the family resources may be spent on the extramarital relationship.
- Depression and the risk of suicide.

- The other partner starting an affair (which leads, to all of the above mentioned problems).
- Children becoming orphans if their parents die of HIV/AIDS.
- Reduced respect between partners.
- Physical and verbal abuse in the family – because of the family conflicts this causes.
- Witchcraft and use of love potions and other concoctions.
- Lack of trust.

Due to the devastating effects that extra-marital affairs might have on the partner and the family, Islam, Tradition and Law accept it as a valid reason for divorce. But they also emphasize the possibility of apologizing and forgiving the partner who has wronged in order to save the family and to prevent its complete breakdown.

Spousal battery - Correctional beating

"Beating is a necessary ingredient of a family." - "Kumenya ndimankhwala a banja." (Malawian proverb)

"As to those women on whose part you fear disloyalty and ill-conduct, admonish them (first), (next) refuse to share their beds, (and last) beat them (lightly) but if they return to obedience seek not against them means (of annoyance) for Allah is most high great above all." (Qur'an 4:34)

"No person shall be subject to torture of any kind or to cruel, inhuman or degrading treatment or punishment. " (Malawi Constitution 19:3)

There are only a few people in Malawi who have never been beaten. As a child, we grow up being beaten to correct our behaviour in school and in the family, as an adult we might be beaten by the police if suspected of committing a crime, or if crying during labour by the nurses in the hospital, or by our spouses, in-laws or co-wives.

The Malawian culture recognises two types of beating: the educational (*kumenya kophunzitsa*) and the violent one (*kumenya kwa nkhanza*). While the first one is an accepted tool of changing somebody's behaviour, the latter is outlawed. During a research by the Lekani Nkhanza Project a woman stated in a focus group discussion: *"When the man slaps you, it means he loves you. He does not want you to go back to your village but that you should just change your behaviour, it could be that he tried several times but you did not listen."*

Even children were of the view that parents have the right to beat them because they need guidance to grow up with good manners. One girl said: *"A child can not grow up without being beaten; it should be beaten so that it does not repeat the same mistake"* (girl child interview partner).

It seems that physical violence is considered an almost unavoidable and unquestioned tool for solving a conflict, or to "teach somebody a lesson". But once beating or slapping is accepted as an educational means, several questions come up:
- At what point does beating start to be violent? Only when blood comes out or bones are broken? That does not seem to be a good indicator as some people beat in a way that leads to severe internal injuries but no visible signs.

- How can members of the society live harmoniously together if one of the most accepted tools for conflict resolution is beating?
- Is beating as a tool for conflict resolution really part of the Malawian tradition or are there other means of conflict resolution?
- Is it legal and tolerated by religion and what means of conflict resolution do those institution consider proper?

Those questions will be discussed by the panellists.

Fac: To begin our discussion, I will hand over to T/A so he can explain to us why beatings occur in a family and then the Sheikh will give us the religious view and then the lawyer will tell us what the law says. Why do beatings occur in a family?

T/A: When somebody in the Yao culture wants to get married, their *ankhoswe* are supposed to meet. They are also supposed to be contacted whenever there is a problem such as spousal battery.

Sheikh: A marriage is supposed to be a place of happiness and harmony, but problems such as pointing fingers or having arguments and many other problems may arise. The Qur'an says when you see that a situation is going out of control in the marriage it is best to call the *ankhoswe*. They should be made up of representatives from the female side as well as representatives from the male side. They should come and advise the couple accordingly and remind them of the importance of marriage so that they can discuss the matter peacefully.

Fac: We have heard that what Islam says is similar to what the T/A said. What does the law say about battery in marriage?

Law: I would like to agree with what the Sheikh said that marriage is a place of happiness. Nobody gets married to their enemy. Marriage is an arrangement whereby a person chooses who they want to spend their lives with. To protect marriage, the Constitution, the highest law of Malawi has put in place laws that do not allow any form of abuse like battery or any other act that makes a person suffer such as treating a family member like a slave.

Fac: I would like to ask the panellists what circumstances may lead to battery in a marriage.

T/A: People in the marriage have an argument because they do not respect one another; this may lead to a situation whereby one beats the other.

Sheikh: Every marriage should have set rules. In Islam, the wife has the duty of taking care of the home and children and to make sure that no undesirable people enter the home. It may happen that the wife disregards or breaks one of those rules which were agreed with the husband using Islamic guidelines. This can make the husband angry and cause the couple to physically attack each other.

There are also other reasons. A wife expects her husband to do nice things for her, to clothe her, feed her and other things because he has taken her from her parents' custody. Maybe the husband is unable to do certain things that she expects of him. Another reason may be that the man goes out a lot. This makes the woman angry and they can start fighting over this.

To avoid those things, Islam has set up guidelines such as patience. The man should be patient; he should avoid getting angry when his wife loses her temper and vice versa. When a person is angry a lot of things can happen; one can be angry to the extent that he kills someone. One thing a person should keep in mind are the words of our prophet Mohammed who said that to prevent oneself from getting angry, one should remember that anger is the work of the devil. He advised that if somebody is angry and he or she is standing then he or she should sit down. If the person was seated then he or she should stand up. So we should all practice patience. If you see that you have failed, then you should go to your *ankhoswe* so the matter can be discussed.

Fac: Can you explain to us what happens in a situation where the woman dresses as required and they attend prayers together, but then during the night we hear that they were beating each other. What could have started the fighting in such a scenario?

Sheikh: As I said before, it is not appropriate for a man to go out until odd hours, sleeping with other women with the wife left alone in the home. When you come home late at night and you are tired and yet your wife is waiting for you. The same thing applies to the women, maybe she goes out and sleeps with another man and comes home and all that time her husband was waiting for her, so they get into an argument and end up fighting.

Fac: Let us now hear from the lawyer if these problems come before her in court and how judgment is passed. We would also like to hear from her how we can help these married couples who are having these problems.

Law: One thing we should remember is that marriage is not a war zone or a place where a person should be miserable. Marriage should be a place of love and happiness.

Somebody, who justifies beating as part of our custom and thinks that the law will protect him, is completely wrong, it is actually forbidden by law. If a wife dies as a consequence of severe beating, the man will be charged with murder, the sentence is either life imprisonment or the death sentence. If you stab or cut your spouse, you will be charged with unlawful wounding which can land you a jail sentence. If you beat your partner up and he or she is swollen or has other injuries you can also end up with a jail sentence. There are so many charges that can be connected to battery.

Therefore we should not hide behind our customs and believe that it is allowed to beat up one's spouse. The Constitution of Malawi has put a law into place which prohibits all customs that encourage abuse. Abuse does not affect the mother or father only, it affects the children as well. Sometimes when the parents fight, they involve the children. When some men get drunk, they start beating up the children for no apparent reason. As a consequence of an argument with the husband in the bedroom, a wife may slap a child. What should be known is that any fighting in a family is a crime according to the laws of Malawi.

Fac: We hear other people talking about educational beating. They mean that by beating their spouse they will be teaching him or her the right way. Is this permitted according to the law of Malawi?

Law: As I mentioned before, the Constitution of Malawi does not permit any type of beating. If your spouse has done something wrong, the situation should not be rectified by beating but instead the matter is supposed to be taken to the *ankhoswe*. There are other institutions that have been set up by the government for couples who cannot resolve issues on their own. They would be in a position to assist. If we are unable to solve the problem, then we should go to court, to our *ankhoswe* or chiefs and get a divorce if necessary and the couple can go their separate ways in good health; our Constitution does not permit people to beat each other under any circumstances.

T/A: There is no law in the Yao culture which allows a husband or wife to beat their spouse. This is *nkhanza* because the abused spouse lives in fear. Beating ones wife is wrong. If the spouse has done something wrong, it is best to go to their *ankhoswe*. It is the duty of the *ankhoswe* to tell the perpetrator that he or she is wrong. Sending the couple to talk to their *ankhoswe* is what we as chiefs have always recommended. If the *ankhoswe* fail to settle the matter then it is forwarded to the chief.

Fac: We have also heard that there are other people who at times say that Islam allows the beating of a wife. Sheikh, please enlighten us on what Islam says about wife battery. Is that a way of educating her?

Sheikh: The Prophet Mohammed said that all people are representatives of the faith and everyone will be judged on judgment day on how they conducted themselves. The mother in the family will be asked by her children if she did conduct herself accordingly. The father will also be asked on how he conducted his teachings to his wife.

When we go to the issue of beating, Islam does not excuse or allow a man to beat his wife nor does it say that this was a way of teaching. If at the beginning when the couple was getting married the marriage was not built on a good foundation then it will not be solid. The Prophet Mohammed says do not marry on the basis that you have fallen in love with her alone because you may marry a woman who is not suitable. The same thing may happen to a woman. She may marry a man who is a wife beater or an abuser in other ways.

The Koran further goes on to say that if there are problems in a marriage, the couple should not engage in violence. They should call on their *ankhoswe* from both sides. They should come together and settle the issue amicably so as to avoid any physical abuse. The man and woman should be civil to one another as they are both human beings.

In short Islam does not permit a spouse to beat the other as a way of correcting him or her.

Fac: I would like to go back to T/A, who is our cultural representative here. T/A, I am Yao myself and I have heard before that some women are told before they get into marriage that in case of problems in marriage such as being beaten, they should persevere. Does this happen here?

T/A: I personally have not heard of any such thing maybe the T/A and chiefs before my time experienced such things.

Fac: After hearing the opinions of the T/A, the sheikh and the lawyer, we would like to invite the general public to ask questions.

Question: What if my husband continuously abuses me physically, whom can I report the matter to?

Law: There are many different options. First of all, you should protect yourself. There are different ways to do this. When you feel that a fight is going to start, you can run away and hide or alternatively go to a friend who stays close by and ask them to come with you and protect you.

There are also times, maybe when your husband comes back from a drinking place, when you know if you respond to your husband in a certain way, you will provoke him. Then you should try not to answer him back and leave any discussion for the following day.

Married people usually have their *ankhoswe*. They should be the first people you talk to. But if you see that the situation does not improve, then there are governmental and non-governmental organisations, that you can go and report to. Some villages in Mangochi have formed a Gender Based Violence committee; they can counsel you or refer you to another institution, for example Social Welfare Department. You can also report to the police. Here in Mangochi, they have a department that deals with problems such as these which is called the Victims Support Unit. When one goes there, they will be able to investigate and see how best they can be able to assist you.

Question: The Sheikh said that in Islam, divorce is not permitted. What should a couple do if they are unable to settle their differences?

Sheikh: I think you did not understand what I said. I said God is not pleased when a marriage ends. Divorce is allowed but that is one of the things that God hates.

Question: My question goes to the Sheikh. What should a man do if the woman says she has the right to do what she wants to the extent that she goes out whenever she wants without telling her husband?

Sheikh: Islam says a wife is not permitted to go out without telling her husband where she is going. When the situation comes to a point that she says she has the right to do anything she wants, then you have serious problems in the marriage. So what you as the man should do is to call a representative from both sides and ask for advice. You may want to ask what should happen if the representatives fail to reconcile the couple, then God permits people to divorce.

Question: My question goes to the Sheikh. I may be living with a man happily and yet we neither had an official religious ceremony nor the traditional one. What can I do?

Sheikh: The answer to your question is very simple. It is not permitted in Islam for a man and a woman to live together before going through the religious ceremony. If the man refuses, you should not agree to live with him as his wife.

Question: The lawyer mentioned that if a spouse has been beaten up, he or she should go and file a complaint in court. I know that you require proof in court. What if the person has been beaten and yet the person does not have injuries, how can you make certain that that person has indeed been beaten up?

Law: If the person files a complaint at the police, they send him or her to hospital to be examined. The medical experts there have a way to tell whether a person has been physically abused or not, even if that person does not show any injuries. They then write a report and send it to us at the court. When we handle the case we rely on the medical report sent to us by the hospital.

A woman can also file a complaint against her husband several days after the beating. In this case she does not have to undergo the medical examination; but here we rely on what the woman herself tells us and if there were any other witnesses who may have seen the beating taking place.

Fac: Before we close our discussions, I will ask the T/A, the Sheikh and the lawyer to give us their closing remarks.

T/A: If in your homes you are being beaten and your parents say you should persevere since they may fear losing whatever they benefit from their son-in-law, this should stop completely because in the end you may lose your life.

Sheikh: What we should do as Moslems, is to take time to learn about our faith. We should encourage our children as well. Once these children as our future leaders learn about their faith I can assure you all this beating will stop. These things are happening because we are Moslems in name only. Maybe you didn't know some of the things we discussed here, but all the information is in the Qur'an. This shows that we are not growing spiritually.

Another issue I would like to mention is that we should individually scrutinize the person we want to make a commitment to. You have to find out more about the person not just base your choice on love. If we do this we will not have many problems in the marriage.

Lastly, beating is not a way of educating a woman or a child.

Law: I would like to repeat that marriage is not a war zone or a place where one should get used to living with an enemy. Marriage should be a place of love. Therefore, the courts and other representatives of the law will primarily attempt to keep the couple together and reinstate the peace.

There are some women who are beating their husbands. Because the men fear being laughed at they leave the problem unreported. The women do the same when they get beaten; they hide their situation and do not report it. They fear that if they report this to court their husband will be arrested and the marriage will be over. So if we want to stop *nkhanza* we should report abuse to the organizations that have been put into place by our government. I will not talk about the husband and wife alone, even children have a right to report abuse.

Fac: What we have learnt here is that beating a spouse is not a right, it is *nkhanza*. We also learnt that beating is not a way of educating someone and that if we continue hiding the abuse the marriage will have endless problems and you may lose you life as well.

Conclusion

As the facilitator already high lighted, neither educational nor violent beating is tolerated by any of the institutions represented. This ban includes men, women and children; none of them should be beaten as an educational measure or as a consequence of anger.

To prevent this kind of violence, the panellists came up with the following suggestions:
- Choose the partner wisely to avoid marrying somebody who later might turn out to be unsuitable or an abuser. Being married to the right person reduces the chances of getting angry and therefore the incidence of *nkhanza*.
- Resort to the *ankhoswe* as soon as a problem arises and not when the beating has already taken place. So the accepted way of conflict resolution for the institutions represented here is through dialogue with the involved parties and the *ankhoswe* as mediators. Their way of counselling is to sit down with the spouses and their families, talk with them and find ways of resolving the conflict and avoiding future ones. They should **not** encourage the wife to persevere in an abusive marriage.
- If the problems continue even after several interventions by the *ankhoswe* and the chiefs, all three institutions agreed that it is better to get a divorce than to remain in an abusive relationship where someone might lose his or her life.
- Try to be patient as a way of anger-management. The sheikh advised that we should move (stand up or sit down) which gives the angry person time to think about what he or she is going to do and to cool down.

- When a person fears that the situation is getting out of control, he or she should run away or seek help instead of trying to resolve the problem and being beaten as a consequence.
- Nobody should remain silent in a violent and abusive relationship but should report the case to the available institutions. The more cases that are reported, the more violent behaviour becomes unacceptable and perpetrators might stop their behaviour for fear of imprisonment.

Denied Sex, Forced Sex and Rape

"When a wife refuses to have sex
Kweche kweche kho!
Bring her behind a big stone
Kweche kweche kho!
Have sex with her
Kweche kwech kho!
She should really feel it
Kweche kweche kho"

„Mkazi akakana
Kweche kweche kho!
Ukokere kumwala
Kweche kweche kho!
Ukachite naye
Kweche kweche kho
Kuti naye amvetse
Kweche kweche kho!" (Malawian song)

"Your women are your tilth, so come into your tillage when and how you choose; but do a previous good act for yourselves, and fear God, and know that you are going to meet Him; and give good tidings unto those who do believe." (Qur'an 2:223)

Any law that discriminates against women on the basis of gender or marital status shall be invalid and legislation shall be passed to eliminate customs and practices that discriminate against women particularly practices such as sexual abuse, harassment and violence. (Malawi Constitution 24, 2, a)

"A satisfactory sexual life is an essential element for the success of a marriage"; every married – and maybe even unmarried – person will agree on that. But that raises the question: What are the standards for a satisfactory sexual life? What some consider as more than sufficient, others might regard as inadequate, it is a very personal issue and varies from person to person. The same person might even change his or her point of view several times within his or her lifetime, depending on age – younger people usually have a greater sex drive than older people. A person's mental state, factors such as tiredness, workload, and stress may have a negative impact on the desire, and a person's hormonal make up can make some people have a higher sex drive than others.

If both partners have different sexual needs then, problems in marriage may start. The one with less drive may feel pressured to perform up to the expectations of the other, while the one with more drive may feel rejected. During a research, men and women consider refusing to have sex as a severe form of *nkhanza* as well as demanding sex too frequently. *"Refusing to have sex with your wife is a very severe form of nkhanza yet that is the reason behind getting married: A person can get nsima and fish from their parent's home and other relatives but they need to have sex with their spouses"* (male interviewee). *"Refusing to have sex with your husband when you have quarrelled or when you are upset is a very severe punishment."* (female interviewee). *"Demanding sex throughout the night without giving the wife time to rest is also a sort of nkhanza."* (male interviewee). Women complained especially that they don't have the same power to demand sex as men do.

It seems to be difficult for partners with different drive to overcome that problem. Some men and women consider an extra-marital affair as the best way out; other men seem to resort to forcing their wives.

But forced sex within a marriage doesn't happen only when the two partners have different sexual needs. It is often used as a punishment for women who are already physically or emotionally abused. Or a husband might use it to humiliate his wife, maybe as a consequence of a long standing quarrel or argument. In such cases, forced sex in a marriage can be worse than rape because it is likely to happen often, because it goes hand in hand with other forms of violence like beating and because it is done by someone they love and trust. In cases such as these, the man's sexual desire are secondary, he merely wants to show his wife that he has the power and that he is in control.

Because the woman might be a victim of repeated forced sex (since she shares a home, and possibly children, with her husband), she may live in constant fear of assault.

If we look at it from that perspective, rape and forced sex are basically the same, in both cases the man forces a woman to have sex without her consent. The only difference is the legal consequences that derive from the status of the woman.

The current law in Malawi promotes the idea that a woman consents to sex with her husband for as long as the marriage lasts. As a result, the law does not regard forced sex in a marriage as rape – because rape is defined in law as sex without consent.

So, the actual law permits forced sex in marriage, but what does religion say? And what is the opinion of the customary law? Under which circumstances is it permitted or outlawed?

Fac: Today, we are discussing forced sex within and outside of marriage. Let us start with forced sex in a relationship, where two people are engaged but not yet married, does this happen?

T/A: Forced sex in such a relationship does happen. When we say "forced sex", we mean an agreement has not been reached by the two people involved. When we look at the Yao custom, forced sex is neither permitted in a relationship nor in marriage.

Fac: Now, who forces whom, is it the man or the woman in the affair?

T/A: Nowadays both men and women can force their partners to have sex.

Law: Forced sex is in two categories. There is the forced sex that happens to an adult and there is forced sex that involves a minor. Forced sex that involves an adult who is not your spouse is called rape. An adult in this case is a person who is above 14 years of age.

When an adult has sex with a minor (a child under 13 years of age) it is called defilement. The law says a child below the age of 13 is not capable of granting consent to an adult to have sex with him or her. At times, because the child may not know what it means to have sex, he or she may agree or even ask an adult to have sex with him or her. Therefore, an adult may be charged with defilement regardless of whether the child had agreed or not.

Another category of defilement is when a person has sex with somebody who is mentally unstable or ill, being either an adult or a child. Some adults are mentally ill to the extent that they do not know what they are doing nor do they understand what is going on around them. Those people may not even know that they are having sex. So, even if they don't refuse, the other person is guilty of having forced the mentally ill person to have sex.

Fac: We will ask the lawyer to clarify this issue of rape so that we understand fully.

Law: If you penetrate the woman, even just a little bit, you have committed rape. Some think that just because they did not ejaculate, they have not committed rape. But the law says: if the tip of the penis has slightly penetrated, as long as there is proof that this was done, you will have committed rape. Some may say I did not commit rape because I wore a condom; if you penetrated when the person involved had refused, then you have committed rape.

Rape also means that, even if you prove in a court that you had a relationship with the woman, you will still be charged with rape because the person you forced sex on is not your wife.

Sheikh: In the Islamic Religion, rape is when you force a woman you are not married to have sex, if it is in a marriage then it is called forced sex. We must make sure we understand the difference.

If you have forced sex with a woman whom you are not married to this is unlawful and it is disgusting. God says in the Qur'an that you must not commit adultery because it is disgusting and evil. In addition to this, if the person has committed rape, then the person has committed two offences; the first one is of conspiracy, the other is of adultery.

T/A: If somebody has committed rape, we as chiefs, according to our guidelines do not call for a tribal hearing; instead we send the accused straight to the Police.

Sheikh: Now in the case of a married couple, every house should have set guidelines that are to be followed. If one partner forces himself on the other, this means that there was no consent. We have to listen to both sides of the story and also find out why the woman refused.

There are times where it is not possible for a man to sleep with his wife and then they must adhere to those rules. For example, every month a woman menstruates; God does not permit sexual intercourse at this time, it is considered a sin. So the sexual act should always be with the consent and agreement of both partners and at the right time to avoid committing a sin.

But to women who refuse without any apparent reason, our prophet Mohammed said: should a man call his wife and asks her to have sex with him, if she refuses for no apparent reason, the angels will curse that woman the whole night until dawn.

T/A: In our culture, it is stated that if the woman is sick or is menstruating, she takes a red strand of beads and puts it beside the bed to show that she is not in a position to have sexual intercourse. If the husband forces her to sleep with him, the woman can go to her *ankhoswe* to report the incident.

Fac: At times, do you get complaints from women that their husbands often refuse to have sexual intercourse with them?

T/A: This does happen. There are plenty of reasons. Sometimes the husbands are drunkards to the extent that they do not sleep with their wives. The wife in this case has the authority to report the situation to her *ankhoswe*. If the *ankhoswe* are unable to resolve the issue then it goes to the chief. We as chiefs then try to resolve the issue by giving them herbal remedies if they are failing to perform.

If it is the woman who is refusing, we as chiefs do not interfere if the woman did not go to her *ankhoswe*. If she goes to the *ankhoswe* we advise them to investigate thoroughly to find out why the woman is refusing. Some women say that when they have sexual intercourse, they feel pain around their belly buttons. In such a situation we look for herbal remedies for them.

Fac: Why do we say that it is *nkhanza* when a spouse refuses to have sexual intercourse with her partner?

Law: A lot of us think that when we enter marriage, we will be entitled to have sex every single day or every hour, but there are a lot of reasons that can make a husband or wife refuse to have sexual intercourse with their spouse.

There are some spouses – men and women – who want to have sexual intercourse with their partners every single day. They forget that their partner is also a human being, at times he or she may be tired and therefore may not be able to perform.

There are some customs that do not allow people to have sexual intercourse at a particular time. For example, when there is funeral in a village, married couples should not sleep together for a few days. Another example is when a girl-child in the family starts menstruation, then the parents should sleep separately for a few days. Another situation is when a woman has just given birth. Some customs stipulate that after giving birth she is supposed to stay at least 3 weeks without having sexual intercourse, other customs say 6 months. In such circumstances, the woman may be physically fit, even if you try and persuade her, she will refuse because she will be following a custom that she believes in.

Another plausible reason could be illness. If a man or woman is ill, they may refuse.

Some men and women start having extra-marital affairs and then they completely neglect their spouses.

Fac: Forcing sex on your partner is bad but refusing to have sexual relations with your partner is also bad. We are saying it is a form of *nkhanza*. What type of *nkhanza* is it? Is it physical or psychological?

Sheikh: Forced sex and rape are *nkhanza*. It is both physical and psychological abuse. What we have to remember is that the main point of a marriage is for two people to live together. They should assist one another.

What I should explain is this part about assisting one another in a marriage. Sexual relations cannot be performed by a man or woman on their own. The act can only be performed when both parties are in agreement. At times it is possible that the man can be aroused and yet the woman may not be at that level. Sometimes it happens that a spouse has climaxed and yet the other has just been aroused. That is a form of abusing the partner.

Fac: The Sheikh told us in detail that it is necessary to engage in foreplay before getting into the actual sexual act, so that both parties are ready, because if this is not done, and one party starts the act before the other is ready, then that means the other person has been forced and this is also an act of *nkhanza*. We will leave it at this juncture though. We will now ask people in the audience to ask any questions they may have to the panellists.

Question: I would like to know what should happen if one party wants to have sex and yet the other party refuses. You are already aroused and yet your spouse says she is tired or angry about other issues. Now you, the aroused person for fear that you may go elsewhere for sexual satisfaction and contract AIDS or maybe you just do not want to commit adultery, what can one do as a man when you have been aroused but your wife is refusing?

Law: As the Sheikh said earlier, before commencing the sexual act, you should know whether your partner has been aroused as well. The way I can answer is that usually a woman knows when the husband wants to have sex. If you have been abusing her the whole day and at night you ask her for sex, then you will start an argument.

Fac: Are you satisfied with that response?

Question: You have partly answered my question. I have been away to the lake on business. Upon my return I find my wife angry because she suspects that I was sleeping with other women while I was away. But, truthfully, I was not doing so. When I ask her for sex, she thinks: "I will punish him". When it is bedtime and you try to touch her, she shows you that she is not interested since she is angry. She is thinking of things that did not actually happen. If you get to the extent that you force her to have sex with you because you want to avoid committing adultery, will such a situation be taken as forced sex in marriage.

Law: The main issue it that there should be a dialogue between the partners to clarify the issues. One reason why she might suspect you of misbehaving is that you have changed the way you perform in the bedroom. During the first months of your marriage you may have had sex daily or even several times in a day. So the woman gets used to this, she knows that a certain period does not pass before her husband has sex with her. After a while you might not perform the same way and she starts to suspect. So you should communicate properly with your wife.

Question: My question goes to the Lawyer. We as men have a lot of needs. We may desire a woman because of the way she is dressed for example she wears mini skirts. So you may be chatting with your girlfriend but at that time you are aroused and then you force her to have sex. What does the law say about such a situation?

Law: Concerning the question that was put forward, these days, there is freedom of dressing, a person is free to dress the way they want to.

If I were to tell you of the cases that are brought to court, most of the victims of rape are decently dressed women. But regarding your question, if she does not consent, you have committed the crime of raping her.

Question: At times it is possible that married people live in harmony and love. You work in the fields together and afterwards you harvest and sell the products. But before the money is budgeted for, the man goes gambling and the wife does not even have a *chitenje*. When he returns, are you wrong to refuse to have sex with him?

T/A: According to the tradition of marriage which came from the ancestors, everything should be done according to certain procedures. When such a thing happens it means he has stolen from you, because when you were working hard on the land, your expectations were that you would improve your home. So when this happens, that means one partner has undermined the marriage.

A marriage should have guidelines, what happens in the marital bed should be left there. Instead of refusing to have sex with your partner, you should go to your *ankhoswe* and report the matter.

Question: At times you may have a disagreement with your husband. When both are upset, is it possible to have any harmony in the family? I would like to ask the men in particular since they are usually the instigators.

T/A: In our culture, it is not considered an appropriate behaviour to ask the other for something when you have a disagreement. Sometimes the women are anxious because the men come home angry. Men often come home tired because they were out until late and then they go straight to bed. The woman then thinks that her husband does not have sex with her because he had already slept with someone else. Often such is not the case. You men, you should sit down and tell your wife that you are tired. When you do so then all will be well.

When we do that "job", we must remember that this is done by the two of you. You should ask for sex when you want it. The women are complaining that their husbands are forcing them to have sex. Forcing your partner is not right because then things go wrong.

Sheikh: A marriage is supposed to be a place of peace and happiness for the two. It can not be proper if you are always shouting at each other, because continuous disagreements pave the way for the disintegration of the relationship.

The first thing to disintegrate is your sexual relationship no matter who has brought the problem into the marriage.

Maybe when the husband is away he may get annoyed or angry with something. He thinks: "When I get home, I will feel better, I will be happy." The same applies to a woman; maybe something has made her angry while she was fetching water. It is imperative that both know that at home you will be happy; none of you should dread what type of atmosphere you will find there.

If you fear to come home, you are not getting along, that means, the "job" in the marriage will not be done.

Question: My question is directed to the Sheikh. You mentioned that that "job" is for two people. So when one partner is ready then there is need for the other to be ready as well. How would a person be able to tell that my partner is now ready?

Sheikh: Everyone knows what happens between a man and a woman in the bedroom, there is nothing to hide. When a person is ready, you can tell and even when you are ready your wife can tell as well. That is why we are supposed to touch the woman. If the woman is not ready and you go ahead and have sex with her, you will cause her harm.

The way you would know, first let me apologize to you ladies and gentlemen, I do not want to offend anyone, is that a woman has fluids that come out when she is ready. When this happens, that means you will be able to enter her without any difficulty.

Question: You said in marriage there is no rape but it is called forced sex. What is worse, forcing your wife to have sex or raping a strange woman?

Law: If you have raped a woman, you have committed a serious offence. You are sent straight to the police because you have broken the law. You will be arrested and the crime is punishable with a lengthy prison sentence.

Question: Some woman can be mentally ill but they look as if they were normal. You may meet one of them and she asks for money and you give her. When you meet her again, she asks for a *chitenje*. Later on you see her expression and you just tell her lets go and have sex and she agrees. If you have consensual sex with her is that a crime?

Law: Let us be honest, you will have committed a serious crime; you will have violated her. I have seen a lot of those mentally ill women who dress well and ask different men for sex. But because they are mentally ill, they do things they would not do if they were normal. It is the illness that causes her to do what she does.

And by the way, why would a decent man in his right mind leave his wife at home and have sex with a mentally ill person just because she is offering her body?

Conclusion

As we have seen, all the three institutions condemn rape and defilement as very severe crimes. The fact that the victim may have been dressed in a short skirt (also a very subjective matter) or is engaged to the perpetrator doesn't diminish his guilt in the eyes of the panellists. They also agreed that, even though it is not punishable by law, forced sex within marriage is something that should be avoided as a way of respecting the spouse. She may deny sex due to biological reasons (menstruation), cultural reasons (birth, funeral in the village) or tiredness. The husband is supposed to accept those justifications, if he forces her, it is considered an act of *nkhanza*.

Disagreement came in when one participant asked about her right to refuse sex after her husband had violated her rights by stealing the fruits of one year's work in the field by spending the money on other women. The T/A suggested that she should not refuse her husbands sexual advances but should have sex with him and then report the case of the spent money to the *ankhoswe*. The statement of the T/A implies that he concedes to the husband the right to use power, that even though he has cheated wife, this is not a valid reason for her to refuse to have sex with him. This opinion is not in line with the one of the other two panellists who emphasised that a necessary precondition for a satisfactory sexual intercourse is the harmony between the couple. Therefore, the partners should treat each other with respect; both should make sure, that the partner enjoys sex as much as they do.

Although not discussed explicitly, the statements of the participants and their emphasis on the need for harmony and mutual enjoyment make it clear, that forcing the wife to have intercourse as a means of demonstrating power and humiliating her is considered as disgusting and as repugnant as rape.

REJECTION AND DESERTION

"Those who swear off from their women, they must wait four months; but if they break their vow God is forgiving and merciful. " (Qur'an 2:226)

"A petition for divorce may be presented to the Court either by the husband or wife on the ground that the respondent has deserted the petitioner without cause for a period of at least three years immediately preceding the presentation of the petition." (Section 5, Divorce Act)

Every married couple faces problems every now and then. Some couples manage to resolve their differences on their own or through the counselling or mediation of the ankhoswe. Others are less lucky and have to resort to divorce as the only option.

Some couples don't even manage to get a divorce; one spouse simply leaves the other and the children; they desert the family. For example, a man who finds that he cannot afford to look after his wife and children may just leave, or a battered woman who fears for her life might run away. Sometimes, a person consults with various members of the primary justice system (such as ankhoswe, religious leaders, or relatives and friends) before making the decision to desert the marriage.

Other couples separate before they even marry, at times a man abandons a pregnant woman without marrying her; he refuses to accept paternity. This case is referred to as rejection.

At first glance, desertion and rejection seem to be a much simpler way of ending a difficult relationship rather than going through the – sometimes lengthy – procedures of a divorce or taking responsibility for an unwanted child and his or her mother. But just as not entering in the marriage with the correct procedures has few perceived positive consequences and a lot of apparently negative ones, the rejection of the pregnant woman, or the desertion of a family also has its repercussions. We will hear them from the panellists:

Fac: We will first ask the T/A what procedures he follows when parents bring their child and say she is pregnant but the father does not acknowledge responsibility?

T/A: The procedure we follow here as Chiefs, Village Headmen, Group Village Headmen and Traditional Authorities is to ask her relatives to try to persuade her to reveal the name of the father. If they fail they ask outsiders. If the man responsible has been identified the parents of the girl inform his parents. They sit down and discuss the issue. If the boy accepts and they agree to marry, the Village Headman has to be notified but he leaves the issue in the hands of the relatives of the boy and the girl.

If the boy refuses the Village Headman refers the case to the Group Village Headman. If the Group Village Headman gets the same results he then hands the case over to the T/A, who can hand the case over to the Magistrates Court.

Fac: Now we would like to know how the same situation is handled under Islam.

Sheikh: When a Muslim unmarried girl is found pregnant, that is a very big problem because Islam says you should not have premarital intercourse.

The Prophet Mohammed said to the young people that whoever can get married should do so because being married will stop the young person from getting attracted to other sex and so the young person will keep their dignity.

Islam forbids an unmarried girl to be pregnant but if it happens the girl is questioned and once she names the father, his relatives are sought. Both parties sit down and discuss the issue so that the child may be raised well and the pregnant girl is also well looked after. Islam states that the two should marry with the aim that the baby is looked after because once they are married it will be difficult for the boy to refuse his responsibilities.

Fac: So our religious representative tries to find out how best to deal with the situation but the people involved remain in the congregation; they are not excommunicated or given any punishment. Let us know what the law of Malawi says when a girl has been found pregnant and the father refuses any responsibility.

Law: Just as the T/A mentioned, when a girl gets pregnant and she is not married, there are procedures that have to be followed to find out who is responsible. When he has been found but refuses, the case is sent to court. There is a law which says that every child should be looked after by his or her parents. If the father is unknown, the child will not know one parent. So the court needs to locate the father of this child. This procedure is in line with the Affiliation Act.

Fac: Why it is *nkhanza* to the girl and to the child who will be born not to acknowledge responsibility?

Sheikh: It is *nkhanza* to desert a pregnant woman or girl because the man will not have the responsibility of looking after the pregnancy and the woman will struggle on her own. Apart from this when the child is born, he or she will not experience his or her father's love and it is the right of that child to receive that love.

Law: There will also be psychological abuse on the part of the girl because she may get depressed thinking of how she will look after a child alone. Maybe she is worried about her parent's reaction to her circumstances. So to end all these problems, the girl may resort to dumping or killing the child which would be a serious crime.

The way such a situation can be avoided is if the boy accepts his responsibility and marries the girl or if he agrees to at least assist financially in looking after the child.

Fac: What should be done to stop such behaviour of boys rejecting girls? What can we do as far as our culture is concerned?

T/A: The Village Headmen, Group Village Headmen and Traditional Authorities should make sure that such cases come before us. If we see that we can not handle the situation adequately, the case should be forwarded to the Magistrates Court. If this is done, then the young ones will know the consequences of their actions.

Fac: Now we have exhausted the first part of our discussions which talked about rejection of a girl when she has been found pregnant and is not married. The second part is about desertion. What does it mean when a woman says her husband has deserted her or when a man says that his wife has deserted him?

Sheikh: In Islam, desertion by either a man or a woman is not permitted.

Desertion may be premeditated or spontaneous. When a man leaves the home and the woman does not know the reason behind the departure or vice versa that is desertion. A man may lie to his wife and say he is going to work and not return, likewise a woman may leave the house saying she is going to visit relatives and not return.

Maybe there has been a disagreement between the couple and then one spouse packs up and leaves. The remaining spouse knows the reason behind the departure of the other spouse. This can be considered spontaneous since it was done in the heat of the moment.

Both are not permitted in Islam. The Prophet Mohammed said it is not permitted to be angry with somebody for more than three days. If you have a problem it is wise to sit down and discuss the issue. If the problem cannot be solved, it is better to get a divorce rather than deserting your partner.

Law: The law says, when a husband or wife deserts their partner that means he or she has relinquished all responsibilities that he or she had before in the home.

An example may be that a man usually provides food and other necessities for his wife. He is the one who usually pays the rent. So when he deserts he will stop doing all these things. In the case of a woman, probably she cooks for her husband, does his laundry all the domestic duties in the house. If she leaves she has relinquished all the duties she performed around the house. In the eyes of the law, desertion is unlawful.

Fac: What may cause a husband to desert his family? Likewise for the wife, what circumstances can lead to such behaviour?

T/A: A wife or husband may desert because of constant disagreements in the marriage. If one party is always in a bad mood this may cause the other to leave since there are things that a wife should do for her husband and vice versa.

Sheikh: There are a lot of reasons that can bring about disagreements in a marriage. When a person marries, they have expectations of what they will get from the marriage.

For example, when we talk about a man, he can do his own washing or his sisters can do that for him. They can also fetch water for him to bathe, cook for him, but there is one thing that they cannot do for him no matter how well they get along. Isn't it? *(The audience agrees).* The sister cannot do that for him nor can a brother do this for his sister. So, if there are sexual problems in the marriage, these may result in one of the partners leaving the home.

Fac: What could the other reasons be? Maybe the situation in the bedroom is just fine.

Law: There are many reasons why a person may decide to leave. The usual reasons are because of *nkhanza.*

At times the man leaves the wife because of her behaviour. Maybe the woman always has bad things to say or is swearing all the time. She does not know how to have a decent conversation with her husband so that he enjoys his time at home with his wife. Perhaps she refuses to cook for him or do anything else for him. Or she embarrasses him; all this can make a man leave his wife. She may also be ungrateful, if he does something nice for her she just swears at him.

At times the man takes himself as the overall in charge of the home and thinks that he has the last say in everything. In such a situation the wife feels as if she has no part to play. So in the end the man does whatever he feels like doing. For example, sleeping out and the wife should not have any say in the matter.

Sometimes the man marries as many wives as he wants. I know that polygamy is legal but he has to inform the wife or other wives. Sometimes the man may spend all his money on other women neglecting his wife entirely. The Sheikh mentioned that the husband may also neglect his wife sexually, this may cause the woman to get tired of the husband and so she leaves. Sometimes the wife gets battered as well. Some men beat their wives frequently and so because the wife fears for her life she leaves. At times the woman just leaves her husband without telling him because she wants to be with other men, maybe because she feels she made a bad choice in the first place, that she may prefer someone else because she feels that if she had chosen this other person, she would have been happier.

So it can be either the man or the woman who deserts the family. At times it happens that they have too many children and so the man feels that he will not be able to look after the children. He fears that he will not be able to feed, dress, clothe and educate them and because of this he packs up and leaves.

Fac: Can children make one of the parents leave the home?

T/A: When the blame is placed on the children it will be because the parents just make them scapegoats. The real problem is between the two parents. They just use the children as an excuse.

Law: From my observations, I know that it is possible that children can be a reason for a man to leave the family and go back to his original home. This may happen due to the custom, particularly in matrilineal societies which says that the children belong to their uncle. So the children don't respect their father. As they grow, they look to their uncle for help and guidance.

In such a case the father does not feel obliged to look after his children or to be responsible for their education. He feels that if he educates them, he will be the loser because he can not decide on their future. This makes the children draw closer to their mother and uncle and they all fight against their father.

In the eyes of the law though, children belong to their biological parents.

Fac: We have seen the reasons underlying desertion in marriage. Now let us find out what the religious perspective is on this matter.

Sheikh: The prophet Mohammed said: "Women are the first source of education of a child." During the early years a child spends most of his or her time with the mother. She is the one who teaches the child to speak politely to people, which hand should be used when eating and that the hands should be washed before eating. It maybe that the father does not live with the family and if the child is not brought up properly, this may cause the father to leave.

The child in turn has the obligation of being responsible for his or her parents. The Qur'an says: "we have given the child to the parents who have carried him from the end to the end". The end means the mother carried the child from the time he or she was conceived until the time of birth and she continued to look after the child as a baby with the hope that the child will do good things for her in the future especially in old age.

As it has been mentioned before, we have cultural beliefs which make us give up our own children and pass them on to people who are not their parents. Other cultural beliefs can harm the child because he or she has not been raised accordingly. It can happen that one day that child speaks inappropriately to his or her father. When that happens the father blames the mother that she did not raise her children properly. He forgets the children are his as well.

It is also possible for the father to brainwash the children so that the children do not respect their mother at all. This can be a reason for the woman to leave her family.

Islam says that it is the duty of the parents to look after their offspring and the child is also obligated to be respectful to his or her parents.

Fac: What happens when the husband or the wife leaves the family?

T/A: When this happens, as a chief, I am responsible to find the person who has deserted their family, force them back home to take care of his or her responsibilities.

We do so because of the problems the family may afterwards. Whether it is the man or the woman who has left the home, there are a wide range of problems facing the deserted spouse: looking after children, providing food, clothing as well as trying to educate the children. All these are difficult tasks to execute single handedly. If one spouse wants a divorce then he or she should say so, then the other one is free to remarry.

Law: When a person is abandoned by their spouse, he or she will feel hurt in different ways, but it usually affects women more. She can not remarry within three years.

If she was financially dependent on the partner, their lives will change for the worse. Some women and children turn to prostitution in order to put food on the table. On the one hand, they may get the necessary money but on the other hand, they may contract sexually transmitted diseases such as AIDS.

Sometimes the one who deserted may become promiscuous. If that individual has problems wherever he or she has been and decides to return, they might transmit any sexually transmitted diseases to the remaining partner.

But it is not only the health of the one who has been deserted, that is affected, but the well-being of the children as well. If there are young children and they end up not having enough food, they may start swelling up because of malnourishment.

Due to the effect that desertion may have on the health and well-being of children, deserting a family with children who are younger than fourteen, is considered a serious crime that is punishable by imprisonment.

Desertion is also grounds for divorce. If somebody has left the family for more than three years, the one who remains has the right to go to court and seek for divorce.

Fac: Now we have heard the reasons that might make somebody desert his wife or reject the pregnant girlfriend and what consequences it has for the remaining family as well as for the person that runs away. We would like to invite you to ask questions.

Question: I would like to ask a question concerning rejection. At times the Chiefs have problems handling such cases. They may be approached by an expectant girl and she tells the Chief who the father is. The man can accept that he is responsible but may not be willing to marry the girl. Instead, he promises to look after her. What would you do in such a situation?

T/A: We as Chiefs would encourage the couple to get married. But if this is unacceptable to them, and the family members then we must ensure that the boy takes responsibility for the child and the mother.

Question: Sometimes a boy is forced to marry a girl he impregnated. He agrees to marry her but he refuses to look after her or to have sexual intercourse with her. What can the girl do in such a case?

T/A: The matter should be discussed by the couple and their *ankhoswe*. If they fail, the best way to deal with such a person is to send him to the Chief where he will receive a referral letter to go to the Magistrate's Court.

Fac: If the matter goes to court, how do you deal with such a person in court?

Law: In case they are not married, the court decides that the boy should refund her whatever money she used when going for antenatal sessions or for the delivery at hospital. If there is evidence that the boy is indeed responsible for the pregnancy, the court instructs the man to pay a monthly maintenance of two hundred and fifty Kwacha. When determining the amount the man's income and the child's need are taken into account.

Fac: Until when and how frequently is this maintenance supposed to be paid?

Law: The amount of not less than two hundred and fifty Kwacha should be paid monthly until the child is eighteen years old and is married. But if the child is eighteen and still at school, the father is responsible until he or she completes their education.

Fac: At the time the father is looking after the child, does this mean the mother should remain single?

Law: A girl who gives birth to a child but is not married to the father can marry whom she chooses and same applies to the man.

Sheikh: To add to this, Islam says that if a man wants to leave a pregnant woman, he should still live with her until she delivers. He is supposed to give her whatever she needs. After the birth of the child, the woman has the responsibility of looking after the child and in turn the man has the responsibility of looking after the woman since she is looking after his child. Further to this, the man should not get jealous if another man wants to marry her. In case she gets married, he should continue supporting his child until it is an adult.

Question: There are men who have a child with a woman they are not married to and they refuse to pay maintenance. He has acknowledged his responsibility for the pregnancy with the sole aim of taking the child when he or she is older. How can you assist a person in such a situation?

T/A: If the man has acknowledged that he is responsible and does not support the child, you should take him to court on the child's behalf. If you don't do so you are infringing the child's rights.

It is a pity that such cases have been rampant here. Girls do not do anything when they get pregnant and the boy acknowledges the pregnancy and yet refuses to support the child. What stops you from reporting the matter to the Chiefs? From now on you should report such cases even if he acknowledges responsibility so that we can give you a referral letter to the Magistrate.

Law: It seems as if we all agree with what the T/A has said that if the man has acknowledged responsibility then he is supposed to support the child

Question: In the villages we have a lot of women who lack financial resources. As a consequence, some girls resort to going to the cities and get involved in prostitution. How would you deal with such a girl if she comes back to the village pregnant?

T/A: The Chief in this situation should ask who the father is and he should be called together with the pregnant girl. If the adequate information is not forthcoming then the fine of one goat applies.

Question: My question is as follows: Let us say I am in a marriage and the uncle, who is the rightful guardian of the children, beats my child. I as the father say that he should not beat my child, that I will discipline the child myself. My wife then questions my right to stop the uncle from disciplining my child and tells me to go back to my village. What can I do in such a situation?

Sheikh: In the religious view, the first people who are supposed to teach and discipline a child are the child's parents. When we talk of parents we mean the father and mother who gave birth to the child. But other people who are not from the immediate family are also allowed to discipline the child when there is need to do so. They also have a role to play in raising the child. So there can be other people outside of the family who discipline the child but primarily it is the parent's duty to discipline their child.

Law: For the woman to say such words, at times it is because of the way the father disciplines the child. Some parents discipline their children in a way that they lose any self esteem. There are some fathers who punish their children severely to the extent that people actually ask if he is the child's father or not.

On the other hand, if the child has done something wrong and the uncle knows about it, he should talk to the father and advise him to talk to his child. The father has the right to discipline his children accordingly so that they grow up to be respectful and responsible citizens.

Question: My question is for our lawyer. In your explanations you have said that if a man has deserted his family and is not supporting them financially then the wife has the right to go to the police and report the matter. I see an element of *nkhanza* there. What if a woman deserts her husband, how will you help him?

Law: If the woman had the responsibility of supporting her whole family, the husband has got the right to go and sue her because he as well as their children depended on her. So now that she has abandoned them, they do not have anyone to look after them. Maybe he does not have relatives to whom he can turn to for help. In such a case, you as the man have every right to go and file a complaint since your wife has left you with a responsibility that you cannot fulfill.

Sheikh: Let me just add a few comments. God has said in the Qur'an that a man and a woman have the same rights. The topic we are discussing here and the questions that have come forward imply that the victims are only women but when it comes to the religious ethics there is no difference whether it is a man or a woman. So its does not matter who has deserted the other, the judgement is the same.

Conclusion
The T/As, the sheikh and the lawyer agreed, that rejecting a pregnant girl or deserting a family with children may have a disastrous impact on the abandoned ones. This may reach to the extent that the girl

dumps her child because she is worried about his or her upbringing, the mother might resort to prostitution to gain the necessary money for the children with all the inherent risks, or the children might possibly suffer from hunger, starvation or lack of other necessary support for their education.

All three institutions agree that both parents should be responsible for the upbringing of the child. Therefore, where children are involved, desertion may actually violate the law. For example: Because the law makes both parents responsible for bringing up their children, when one party deserts the other and doesn't provide support to their children, they could be committing a criminal offence. Under sections 164 and 165 of the Penal Code, it is a criminal offence for a parent or guardian to desert a child under the age of 14.

But desertion does not only impact on the children or the remaining partner alone; it also has consequences for the deserter. Neither traditional, Islamic nor Malawian law recognize desertion as a legal option for ending a marriage – that is, the parties remain married even though one party has deserted the other. As a result, neither party may marry again (except for men in polygamous societies) nor may they demand maintenance from the other. If they want maintenance for themselves, they will need to get a separation order or divorce – as dealt with below

Desertion is also grounds for divorce in both customary law marriages and marriages under the Marriage Act. Anyone thinking about it should be aware that their partner may divorce them as a result.

So, the negative consequences of rejection and desertion are:
- Desertion does not legally end the marriage.
- The deserter may be committing a crime if they fail to support children under 14 or if they steal the children.
- The person who deserts the other cannot get maintenance.
- Desertion is grounds for divorce.
- Raises anxiety amongst relatives and friends.
- Can lead to an increased risk of HIV/AIDS.
- Promotes extra-marital affairs.

But despite all the negative impacts desertion or rejection may have for the remaining partner, it may be the only way out for some people. For example:

- Where a partner is very violent and will not allow their partner to seek help from either the formal or informal justice system.
- Where they have tried using both the formal and primary justice structures without success. For example, an ankhoswe may ask a wife to obey her husband and put up with beatings and sexual abuse.
- Where there is severe psychological violence (for example, where one of the parties uses witchcraft against the other).
- Where a person's life is being threatened. For example, where one of the parties is being forced to have unprotected sex and there is a real fear that the other party is infected with HIV

DIVORCE AND PROPERTY

"A husband is like a child, he can marry whenever he wants without deeply thinking about it." – "Mamuna ndi mwana – atha kukwatira nthawi yinda yiliyonse." (Malawian proverb)

"If you fear a break between the two, appoint an arbitrator from his people and an arbitrator from her people. If they both want to set things right, Allah will bring about reconciliation between them. Allah knows all, is well aware of everything." (Qur'an 3:35)

"Women have the right to full and equal protection by the law, and have the right not to be discriminated against on the basis of their gender or marital status which includes the right on the dissolution of marriage to a fair disposition of property that is held jointly with a husband." (Malawi Constitution 24.1.b.i)

Divorce is a final and permanent solution – it ends the marriage completely. If the couple wants to reunite again, they must remarry. In the foregoing dialogues the consensus between the representatives of the three institutions it became obvious, that divorce has serious consequences for all people concerned. One party normally has to leave the house; therefore the children may lose contact with one of their parents and vice versa. It can involve a lot of anger and pain on both sides. For many people, divorce goes against the social, cultural and religious norms. Therefore, divorce should be the last resort when all other options for reconciliation – intervention of the ankhoswe, chiefs or religious leaders – have been tried and all attempts to resolve the issues have failed.

During the previous dialogues it also became obvious, that no divorce can be granted without a good reason, known as the grounds for divorce. It was agreed, that a divorce will only be granted if at least one of the grounds is present.
- Adultery
- Either party can no longer fulfil their duties in the marriage
- Desertion
- Beating
- Cruelty/There is *nkhanza* within the marriage

- Failure by a husband to provide a house or take responsibility for looking after his family
- Failure to support or provide for the family
- Refusal to have sexual intercourse without any reason for a long period
- Failure to take care of or look after a partner who is sick, injured or has become incapacitated
- Irreconcilable differences or irretrievable breakdown of the marriage. This is where the parties have drifted so far apart or the marriage has broken down to such an extent that the parties simply no longer want to be married

But even if one or more of the above mentioned reasons are valid for a couple, they can not decide on their own to get divorced, certain procedures have to be followed. During these procedures important issues will be decided like the division of the property, the custody of the children and – if applicable – maintenance.

Traditionally, the property is divided between male and female property, according to who uses it and who might have acquired it. While this division was very useful in former times, when people didn't own very much more than cooking pots, buckets and baskets or hoes and axes, nowadays, where people own bicycles, TVs or radios, this way of division brings severe problems to the family. How do you determine if belongings are male or female? For example the radio is used by both partners so who will get it? The husband might have bought it in the shop, but to get the money he sold the maize both of them planted in their garden. Additionally, the wife might have cooked for him, washed his clothes, cleaned the house and prepared his bath so that he was able to work fulltime in the garden while she was farming part time.

In matrilineal areas, there is one more reason for serious conflicts: the *chikamwini* system whereby the husband leaves his home village and settles in the village of the wife. All of the important property in the family (such as land, the house and large household items) falls under the control of the brother of the wife, the *mwinimbumba*. The husband does not own the land he lives on or any of the matrimonial property. After divorce, the husband may have to leave the land and the children and return home – even if he built the house using his own money.

Husbands who live in their wives' village usually remain strangers whose only duty is to provide children for their wives' families, since their children are considered to belong to the *mwinimbumba*.

During the discussion, the panellists will deal briefly with the issues of grounds for divorce, and then explain what the correct procedures for divorce should be and finally they will discuss at length the question of property division.

Fac: We first would like to ask the participants to summarise briefly the acceptable reasons for divorce.

Law: The reasons that are considered to be adequate in court are: When there is proof that the husband or wife has committed adultery or a spouse has abandoned the other and does not look after the family any more. We also mentioned that usually our marriages should have ankhoswe, who are responsible for the couple and should help the couple discuss any problems they may have and also try and find a solution.

Sheik: The Qur'an says if there is a problem in a marriage, representatives for both the male and female sides should investigate the matter and come to a conclusion if the reasons or problems in the marriage warrant a divorce, for example, if the couple fights constantly to the extent that people fear that they will kill each other, or if whenever there is a problem in the marriage one spouse threatens to commit suicide. These may warrant a divorce because a life or lives maybe in danger. Marriage is not slavery.

Fac: I will ask the Sheik if the couple fails to produce children, is this a valid basis for divorce?

Sheikh: I will ask a rhetorical question to everyone here: If the couple is unable to have children, whose fault is it? If the couple is unable to have children no one should point a finger at the other because of this, the problem may be with either the man or the woman.

Failure to produce children is not a valid ground for divorce at all. Islam says a marriage can end in divorce if there are irreconcilable differences. Witnesses are supposed to be available which means whatever problems the couple is facing will have been discussed at great length by both the female and male side and a conclusion has been reached that there is no other solution to the problem apart from divorce.

Not being able to have children is not a problem that can not be solved. There are herbalists that can be approached in the villages who can assist or even at hospitals. It should also be kept in mind that children are a gift from God. It is up to Him to grant this gift at whatever time he chooses.

He gives us those gifts just as he may give us other material things such as monetary wealth, cars and other such things. All these are acquired during marriage. It is highly unlikely that you will ask for a divorce just because you have been married for years and you have not managed to acquire a car. We can only ask God for what we want but it is up to Him when and if He will grant us what we have requested.

T/A: It is true that not being able to have children in a marriage is not a basis to get a divorce. There is no one in their right mind who would get married in the name of having children. A person gets married because they want a partner to help him or her with the things that are missing in one's life just as it is said that a man and a woman shall be become one. They will no longer be separate people. So if one of them no longer wants to be a part of the relationship, it is up to the two to separate.

Fac: What procedures are followed which ensure that both people go their separate ways amicably?

Law: People do not just go their separate ways but they have to follow certain procedures which have been but in place by the law.

The procedures that should be followed vary according to what type of marriage it was since we have different types of marriages in Malawi. A traditional marriage can only end through the *ankhoswe*. If they fail to settle the matter, it is referred to the Chief and if that fails as well then the matter goes to court. The same applies if the marriage was officiated in a church. The church elders have to be informed and if they fail to resolve the issue then the couple goes to court.

When two people are in a marriage that is recognized by law, procedures set by the law have to be followed. A couple should not just go their separate ways without following these procedures.

T/A: The right way would be for the couple to call on other people to help them with whatever problems they have and then after discussing the matter, the people who had been called can judge where things stand between the two and take it from there.

Sheikh: The Prophet has said if the husband wants to separate from his wife, he might do so, but he should continue living with her in the same house for a certain period. The Qur'an in Chapter 2 verses 126 and 127 says that if the man has a problem with his wife to the extent that he does not communicate any more with her, he should not continue with this behavior for more than three months. If they decide to reconcile, God will show his mercy and will forgive them. If they decide to divorce there is still a prescribed time that the couple should stay in the same house before the wife can go out and get married again and vice versa. In case the woman is pregnant, they should both know it before the wife leaves. So this period is up to four months, thereafter the couple is free to divorce.

It is emphasized that even if you live separately but under one roof, you should still continue providing for your wife just as you did before. If you do not look after the woman she may stray, the husband might do the same. This may be disastrous because during these months, the couple may change their hearts and decide to reconcile and then one of them brings a sexually transmitted disease into the home.

Fac: Now we have understood the formal procedure, but people often quarrel about property. Therefore, we would like to understand what type of property a family usually has.

T/A: There are different types of property. This can be furniture, pots, pans, beddings, radios, and televisions. These can be considered as household goods. Then we have children. They can also be considered as property, especially in our culture here because when we get married, we will not have had any children.

Fac: Now what property does the man of the house own and what property belongs to the wife?

T/A: It is possible that before a man gets married he goes to South Africa to work or get education and so he may have some property such as furniture, television, beddings and the like, but probably he will not have any children. It is also possible that a man marries when he has no assets at all. So the property he had before is his and the property that he acquired after marriage belongs to the couple. When a situation arises that the property has to be divided, there is a way to deal with it.

Sheikh: The way the T/A has explained, it is not really different from what our religion says. Maybe we may just add that at times it is possible that a man can marry a woman who has wealth and property while he may not have any assets at all.

Now, when we go into our culture, the woman will say she has her property as a woman. When women say this it is most of the times to their disadvantage because the property they consider theirs is normally kitchenware or other things that have little value. But she feels that items she uses daily like buckets and kitchenware belong to her. When she looks at things like a panga-knife or tools used to make sculptures she takes these things as if they belong to the man because she is unable to use them. When the woman says she is leaving, she packs all the kitchenware so that the husband will have nothing to cook in.

But in a marriage, there is no distinction between what belongs to the woman and what belongs to the man. If they have acquired the assets together, then the property belongs to both of them. If the woman found some assets in the home when they got married, the man has a larger share of the property but because the wife has been living with him, she will also have a part of that property. The same applies if the man married a woman who had assets. The larger share of the property in general will belong to the woman, even if she is to die, the man will be entitled to a share of the property because he was married to that woman. If they started from scratch together, that means everything belongs to both of them.

T/A: The way we used to live long ago, when we talked about property, we meant things like baskets used for sifting maize meal (malichero), or buckets used for fetching water (ndowa). At that time we did not have District Commissioners so when the time came to divide the property, it would be divided as follows: if there were two hoes, one would be taken by the wife and the other by the husband but when it came to the baskets, the woman was entitled to those. The man would not take any of those and when it came to the tools used to make sculptures, those belonged to the man. Nowadays we say the property belongs to the couple or we can say we can divide the property fairly because they will have acquired the assets together

Fac: In the home, is there property that belongs to a woman and some that belongs to the man?

Law: There is always a clear distinction that some items belong to the man and some things belong to the woman to the extent that a male child would not touch the stuff that is considered to belong to his mother nor would a girl touch things that belong to her father. Things like the stick used by the man when hunting or the axe which he uses for cutting trees or for making sculptures, such items belong to the man. Should they divorce, the woman will not request such an item since it belongs to the man. The other things that may be considered as strictly belonging to the man can be his clothes, the woman would not ask for them. What would she do with them?

When we talk about the woman, we can talk about items such as her clothes, kitchenware or baskets, those belong to the wife.

Apart from these items, there are other assets that may be considered as general items. For example a television, we cannot say that it belongs to the wife or to the husband. Things like radios or beds: they are used by the whole family.

Fac: Let us look at this scenario. I can go to the market and buy a panga-knife for my husband because I know he needs one. I will not use it but I will buy it. In such a situation who is the owner of the panga-knife?

T/A: In case one of the couple **dies**, the panga-knife that has been bought by the wife will be given to the surviving spouse by whoever oversees the distribution of the assets. But if it is a matter of **divorce**, the woman will take the panga-knife because she bought it on her own.

Sheikh: The Qur'an does not differentiate which items belong to the man or to the woman except for things such as clothes. Male clothes belong to the man even if the wife bought them and vice versa. Distribution of clothing is not even discussed as opposed to things that were used by both of them such as bicycles, cars, television and radios.

Fac: Now, if a man buys his wife a dress or a *chitenje* they automatically belong to the wife even if she did not buy them. Sometimes it happens that a man tells his wife he wants all the clothes he bought for her back and gives them to the new woman he intends to marry after divorce. Is this an accepted behaviour?

T/A: That is not right for the man to take things that he bought for his wife, for example items such as underwear. There are some men who do this. They shout at the women and then forcefully take underwear that he bought for her but when such issues reach our hearings, we tell them that it is an extremely wrongful thing to do. Anything that he bought for her even if it is a day before the separation is hers. We must emphasise that any items of clothing bought for the woman belong to her and vice versa.

Law: To add to this, when we talk of property that has been bought for one partner by the other, the minute I do this, I have transferred ownership. Whatever I will have bought will no longer belong to me but to my partner whom I have bought the thing for. It is not right to take the property back because you have a disagreement. If we do this will be an act of *nkhanza*.

Fac: So, personal items belong to the one who wears or uses them and the property in the home belongs to the couple. What happens when the couple gets divorced?

Sheikh: If the people are getting a divorce, there is the property in the home that is used by all the people in the family. For any property that the woman found in the house when they were getting married, it is up to the man to share it with his wife. The same applies to a man.

If he found property in the house, then it will be up to the woman to share this with the man. This all depends on the owner of the property if they want to share it with the other person and taking into account how long they have been together.

But the property that they have acquired while they were together is divided equally between the two. Sometimes property is bought and the owner may put it in their name or the man may build a house for his wife. But if there is property in the house that does not belong to anyone in particular, it must be divided fairly between the two people. The Qur'an says the woman has the same rights as the man.

Law: According to the law, when it comes to dividing the property, the female belongings used by the wife will go to her, the property that belongs to the man will go to him. The property that they have acquired together and that has been used by both people such as beds, lounge suites, radios, televisions, are divided equally by the lawyers. For example if there are two beds, each will get a bed.

When dividing the property, the court also takes into consideration the reasons for divorce. Who is at fault? It may be possible that the couple acquired the property together but maybe the wife wants a divorce because she got involved with a rich man and now rejects her poorer husband. Somebody who has done such a thing should not expect to get a share of the property to take to the new home. I just wanted to clarify this point because there may be some women here in the audience who may decide that they will leave their husband today and get half of the property. Or maybe the men might think that they want to move in with another woman so they can just leave the wife and get half of the assets.

Usually the one who has wronged his or her partner gets less than the innocent one. In case of desertion, it is very possible that you will lose everything.

The chief had mentioned that children are also considered as property since they are born during the time the couple was married. When the court decides who should take the children, they take into account who will be in the best position to raise the children so that their rights are not violated. If it is the man who is the suitable candidate, he will be granted custody of the children so that he gives them a good education and they can have a bright future. If the man has a lot of money but his behaviour is questionable such that it is doubtful that he will be able to raise them to become respectable citizens, the children will be given to their mother. However he will still have to support them financially. The child is also given a chance to say which parent he or she feels they would want to live with.

Fac: We have heard that the property that belongs to the woman such as clothes and baskets go to the woman. Axes and such things go to the man. The other assets such as radios, televisions, bed, chairs, are shared equally between the two because they will have acquired these during the time of their marriage. When it comes to children, we have been told that the children go either to the mother or father depending on whom the court considers the best parent for them to live with. The children do not go to their uncle.

Question: Let us say when a couple got married and the man paid a bride price (*lobola,*) if this is the case then that means the children belong to the man. Who then gets the children when the parents want to divorce and they take the matter to court.

Law: The Constitution, which is above all other laws and customs, says if a couple has children together, they belong to both. The children belong to the two people who gave birth to them. If they are getting a divorce, both parents are still expected to look after their children. So in the example you gave, court may rule in favour of the woman irrespective of the fact that a bride price was paid, just because they consider her as being more suitable to raise the children. If the woman is in a better position to look after the children, then you should allow her to do so even if you paid a bride price for her.

Custody does not mean that the children **belong** to the one who looks after them. The other person has the right to come and see the children so that they know both parents. Divorce should not infringe on the right of children to grow knowing both parents, divorce should not deprive the children the right to be looked after by both their parents.

Question: My question goes to the Sheikh, a married couple may be together for years and then the wife is found guilty of adultery. What happens on the issue of distribution of property in such a situation?

Sheikh: Your question may seem to be one but there are two factors to be considered here. One is that the woman is guilty of adultery, secondly the division of the property on account of the divorce being granted on the basis of the woman's infidelity. The first thing I can say is, if a woman has been caught committing adultery that is one ground on which divorce may be granted. But this cannot be used as a reason to deny her a share of the property, because the divorce itself is punishment enough. It would not be right to do so.

Question: If you have always been wealthy even at the time of marriage but then later on the woman leaves you. What happens?

Sheikh: When distributing the property, the reason for divorce is also looked into. So if the woman married him just because he is wealthy and is now divorcing him because she expects a share of his property, then she should not expect to get anything.

Law: My advice is that before you marry you should be careful who you marry because some women are very clever. They pretend to love a man because he is wealthy. Sometimes women actually go to the extent of fighting for him. Before accepting a proposal, some women first look at what assets he has. Does he have a television, a radio, does he own a car? The way he looks, does he have money, and will he provide a lavish lifestyle? So at times the woman gets married to the man but then she finds out she does not have as much access to his property as she thought she would. As a consequence, she tries and finds excuses so that she gets some of the property.

Question: Firstly I would like to say that I am surprised that we women are not coming forward to ask any questions and yet we are the ones who mostly get abused in marriage. So I have seen that it will be best for me to ask my question on behalf of the women here. My question goes to the T/A. It may happen that when you get married and as a couple you start with nothing and you start farming or get into the business selling fish. As time goes, you accumulate assets.

Then the husband, according to our culture here wants to have another wife or two. So it happens that when he gets married to another woman, he takes the property you have in the house and takes it to the new wife. T/A, when such a situation is brought to your attention, how do you assist a woman in this predicament?

T/A: Following the traditional law, we do not allow the husband to take assets from one wife to another. He should just go there as he is. If he does not have a blanket, it is better he borrows money from the current wife because in the first place he is supposed to ask for permission from the first wife to take the second wife. If she agrees, then he should also borrow money to go and buy whatever he needs for the new marriage. He should start afresh with the other wife so that they can get to the same standard of life that he has with the other wife.

Law: Marriages under traditional law allow polygamy but whatever has been bought for one wife is not supposed to be taken from her and given to another. Even if you are already married, some women try and get your attention because they have seen how well you look after your wife or they may have seen what assets you have in your home. When the younger wife in court asks for property that belongs to the first wife, it becomes evident that she married the man for his wealth. If a man has two wives and one of the wives wants a divorce, she should ask for the property that is in the house she lives in not what is in the other wife's house.

Question: My question is, if a man is wealthy and he moves around with a lot of different women and so gets infected with HIV. The wife fearing that she may get infected asks for a divorce. In such a situation, who gets the property?

Law: The reason for divorce should be because the husband is continuously unfaithful. Adultery is an acceptable ground for divorce. Even if she does not know if her husband has AIDS, she has the right to fear for her life because of her husband's promiscuous behaviour. If the grounds for divorce is adultery, she will be entitled to a fair share of the property.

Question: You said if people become estranged, this should not continue for more than four months, the situation should be clarified by then. What if they should decide to get divorced after the fourth month and then the woman discovers that she is one month pregnant? How will it be known if the ex-husband is the father?

Sheikh: I think I mentioned that if a partner becomes estranged the couple should not live in separate houses, so if the wife is pregnant it is known by then. During the four months the couple should not have any sexual intercourse. If they do have sexual intercourse at anytime, the separation should end there.

If they want to continue the separation they should start counting from the time they had the sexual encounter. The main reason behind this is to know whether a woman is pregnant or not. It is not acceptable that you have sexual intercourse today and then the next day you tell your partner that you want to leave because the required four months have elapsed. Are you still under any form of separation if you had sexual intercourse the previous night?

Question: My question goes to the lawyer. A couple has been living together for 10 years. When they separate, do they just leave each other without any formalities just because it was never made official? Is this type of arrangement considered as a marriage?

Law: According to the Constitution of Malawi permanent cohabitation is now considered an official marriage.

So if a man takes a woman and lives with her and sleeps with her, you go to church together, people see you as man and wife and the way you live in the house is the way a married couple does then you are considered a married couple. If a problem should arise and you want to divorce, the court will treat you as a married couple. So if there are any people here in a situation such as this one, know that in the eyes of the law, you are officially married even if the Yao culture does not says so.

Question: A man marries and they have several children. When the man gets old, the woman says she wants a divorce because she has found an eligible younger man?

Law: All marriages no matter where they are officiated are done on the premise that the couple wishes to be together for the rest of their lives. When a couple comes to court and wants a divorce, adequate reasons should be given. A reason such as the one presented by the gentleman here is not adequate.

Sheikh: In short I will say religion can not permit divorce when there is no valid reason. Religion says that when a marriage is being officiated, there should be witnesses. The same applies with divorce. The witnesses should investigate if the reasons given are plausible for the couple to divorce. Old age is not a reason that warrants a divorce.

Question: How can a couple be assisted when the parents interfere especially in a situation whereby there may have been problems in the marriage in the past and the couple resolves the matter and yet the parents insist on the couple divorcing?

T/A: It is not proper for parents to interfere in the marriage of their children. If this happens then the ankhoswe should intervene because their duty is to make sure no one interferes with that marriage. If anyone interferes with the marriage then that person should be reported to the Chief. If that person persists then he or she should be sent to the Group Village Headman. If that also fails then that person will be sent to the Magistrate's Court.

Question: How can you assist some of us who are in a marriage with stepchildren? When these children are growing up, we find ourselves in a situation whereby we are unable to discipline the child. At times their mother does not allow me to discipline the children. Is this not abuse?

T/A: According to our culture, once you are married, you have the authority to raise and discipline the children. Disciplining children requires both parents. If the children have done something wrong, the parents should sit down with them and discipline them accordingly. Perhaps sometimes one parent may abuse the child when disciplining him or her and that may be the reason why the mother forbids the father to do the disciplining. What is supposed to happen is that children should not be treated differently whether they are stepchildren or your own.

Law: As we explained before, marriage is a very important aspect of everyone's life. We also said that once a couple is married, it means that all the step- and biological children now belong to both parents. So, as a parent of the children, the stepfather has the responsibility of making sure that the children are raised accordingly and that they grow up to be responsible adults. At the same time, the parents should make sure that counselling is in the best interests of the child.

Question: My question is: A marriage with children ends and the woman or both get remarried. Then the woman prevents the biological father from supporting or visiting his children, how can the law assist this man?

Law: What the man can do is to go to court and report the situation. When the court deals with cases that involve children the main aim is to find out what is in the best interest of the child. The situation therefore will be scrutinized to see if the father's support is beneficial or detrimental to the upbringing of the child.

A problem that we face in our country is that when a traditional marriage ends, custody of the children is automatically awarded to the mother. The court though, does take tradition into account when awarding custody but the main thing they look at is in which environment the child will be well raised.. So in a situation such as this one, if the court feels that the children will be better off with their father, the court may rule in his favour.

Sheikh: Just to add on this, Islam says that the responsibility of looking after a child lies with the father so the mother does not have a right to say that she does not want the father to support his children. The same applies to a mother changing the surname of a child because they are divorced; this is wrong since the child has a right to know who his or her biological father is.

Question: I come from Mulanje. When I came here I got involved with a woman who had three children. We got married and after eight years we had three children. She then said that I should get circumcised or else we should get a divorce. I went for circumcision but after a year she said she wanted a divorce. How can you assist me?

T/A: When you look at this situation to me it seems the woman has a hidden agenda so what I can recommend is that you take her to the Chief so that she explains her reasons and reveals the real reason behind her request to get divorced so that when you leave her you will know what the reason was.

Question: I come from Thyolo. I came here as a young man and married here. We have a son together and I raised and educated him. Later on my wife committed adultery and we divorced. After completing his education, my son has had opportunities to go to England. My ex wife remarried. My son sends things that are supposed to be given to me but my ex wife gives them to her new husband and discourages my son from sending anything to me. If I go to court and file a complaint in court will this be wrong?

Law: The problem is proving that your ex wife has broken the law. What I can see is that there is a misunderstanding between your ex-wife and yourself. My best advice is for you to go to the Chief so the matter can be discussed or you can go to your congregation so that they can remind your ex-wife that you played a role in the birth and bringing up of your son.

Conclusion

The panellists discussed questions regarding valid grounds for divorce, appropriate procedures and property division.

Contrary to what happens very often in the villages, the sheikh and the T/A agreed, that infertility is **not** an acceptable reason for divorce as children are a gift of God. Infertility should either be treated with herbal or other medicines or accepted as God's will.

When it comes to the **right procedures**, the T/A, sheikh and lawyer agreed, that the couple should first approach the ankhoswe for assistance. If they fail, the matter should be brought to the chief. If both parties agree, he can end the marriage, otherwise he might refer them to the group village headman and from there they go to the magistrate court. If the marriage was officiated by church elders, they must also be informed.

Islam has one additional requirement: Before the divorce is granted, the couple must live together for three or four month without having intercourse to find out if reconciliation is possible or if the wife is pregnant. During that time the husband must provide for his wife, afterwards both are free to remarry.

While tradition and religion do not recognize cohabitation as marriage the Constitution does. So if such a couple wants a divorce, they first need a court to rule that the relationship was in fact a marriage by repute and permanent cohabitation. Afterwards, the court will grant a divorce. If it is granted, the court can make orders about the distribution of property, and about maintenance and custody of children.

Regarding the **division of property**, the following was accepted by all parties:
- Personal belongings like cloth, underwear or working utensils like pots, baskets and axes remain with the spouse that uses them regardless who bought them.
- Property that one of the spouses acquired before getting married remains with that spouse. Islam points out, that the one who owns it, might decide to give the other one a fair share, depending on the length of time they have been together.
- All the other property should be divided fairly and equally between both partners.
- The one regarded as having caused the breakdown of the marriage, should get less or nothing, depending on the case.
- In a polygamous marriage, each wife has her own property. When it comes to a divorce, no wife can ask for the property of her co-wife. The husband is also not allowed to take things out of the house of one wife and give it to the other.

Regarding the **custody of children**, the following was agreed:
- The sheikh and the lawyer agreed that the children belong to both parents and not only to one or the uncle. Forbidding the child from seeing his or her parent would deprive the child of his or her birthright. This means that the father in the

chikamwini system also has a right to see his children after divorce.
- The wealthier spouse is obligated to pay maintenance to the ex-spouse and their children

Property Grabbing

"You don't have to wait for somebody to pressurize you to give in, because a person who wants peace just gives in." – "Patse patse mkulanda mwana wamfulu anapereka yekha." (Malawian proverb)

"Do not devour one another's wealth by false and illegal means" (Qur'an 2:188)

"Any law that discriminates against women on the basis of gender or marital status shall be invalid and legislation shall be passed to eliminate customs and practices such as ... deprivation of property; including property obtained by inheritance." (Malawi Constitution 24.2.c)

The practice of taking property away from someone when their spouse dies, or forcing them to return to their original village and to leave their homes and property behind, is very common in Malawi. Like rape and spousal battery, property grabbing is considered *nkhanza* and it is a crime under Malawian law. Property grabbing is usually done by the relatives of the deceased spouse and can take various forms.

- During illness
  This usually happens when one partner is very sick and it is clear that they will soon die. The person's relatives start selling or taking property away from their husband or wife.

- Immediately after death
  During this period, the surviving spouse is most vulnerable. Relatives take advantage of this to get as much property as they can. It is usually women who fall victim to this.

- Making the surviving spouse move away
  Relatives force the surviving spouse to leave the family home and take over the home and household goods. This can happen when the family was living away from either the wife's or the husband's ancestral home. It happens to men in matrilineal societies, and to women in patrilineal societies. When the surviving spouse is forced out, they usually have to leave most

of their property (except their personal belongings) and even their children behind.

- Pretending to be the widow or children
Relatives of the deceased man sometimes get someone to impersonate the widow or child of the deceased to claim death benefits. This deprives the real widow and children of what they are entitled to.

Property grabbing usually takes place **before** the property has been distributed by whatever structure has the power to distribute it.

In other cases, people grab property **after** a proper decision has been taken because they believe that they are entitled to it as customary heirs regardless of what the Wills and Inheritance Act says.

Anybody can be a **victim** of property grabbing. For example, widowers often have their property grabbed in matrilineal societies and sometimes in patrilineal societies too.

However, widows are much more likely to experience property grabbing than widowers. Children are almost always the victims of property grabbing.

Both men and women are **guilty** of property grabbing. In both matrilineal and patrilineal societies, it is usually done by uncles, brothers, parents and sisters of the deceased. In matrilineal societies, nephews are also sometimes the perpetrators of property grabbing.

People who are responsible for distributing property (who are almost always men related to the deceased) have also been known to take part in property grabbing.

Although it is illegal, property grabbing happens very often. So the following questions arise:

- What are the different opinions of the three institutions about who should inherit what?
- Is there any justification for taking away more property from the survivor than one is entitled to?
- What do the representatives of the three institutions consider as the effects of property grabbing?

In the following dialogue, the participant will try to answer these questions.

Fac: Before we start discussing the issue of property grabbing, we should identify who owns the property in the household.

T/A: What I can tell you is, how it used to be in the Yao culture. When a man married, he would take his wife and they would farm or get into business thereby accumulating assets and have children. The property is owned by the two people who worked to buy the assets. If a husband or wife died the remaining spouse would inherit everything. But that is not how it is these days. Nowadays when a man dies, his relatives immediately take the property and divide it amongst themselves. There are many cases of property grabbing that are brought to the courts.

Fac: What happens if one dies, who can come and claim the property?

T/A: In the Yao culture, when someone dies there is a ceremony that is performed. During this ceremony (sadaka), the male and female sides come together. After the ceremony, the two sides meet and distribute the property. They take into consideration if there are children left. If a car has been left behind then they might leave it to the children. If they feel that the in-laws should get something then they will give it to them. What is left untouched are the personal belongings of the remaining spouse. They may feel that some of the property should be sold but all this is supposed to be done in agreement.

Fac: We have been told that if a person dies, the distribution of property is done by the relatives. So who are the bereaved?

T/A: These will be the relatives from both the male and female sides.

Sheikh: According to Islam, the property that is in a home when both are alive belongs to both of them. The difference is in authority of the property. If the man is the one who acquired the property, then he will have authority over it. He has the right to give anyone he chooses any of the property that is in the home,

When one dies, God gives the remaining person a share of the property. For example, if the man dies, the woman who has been left behind will be entitled to a share of the property. Property grabbing is happening if one who takes the property he or she is not entitled to.

According to Islam the one to be considered first is the orphan, a child under the age of fifteen. Wife or husband will not have the same consideration as an orphaned child but everyone is entitled.

For example, if a man dies and leaves a wife, a son and a daughter, then the three surviving family members and his parents are the ones who are entitled to the property. The children will inherit the main part, while the wife and his parents get less. In this case, his brothers, sisters, uncles and aunts are not entitled to anything because there are children who have been left behind.

If there is no wife or child, then the other relatives can have the property. So if the uncle or aunt comes to the bereaved family with children and takes something, then it will be property grabbing because he or she is not entitled

A son is entitled to half of the property but if there are many children they will share until they have distributed at least two thirds of the property. A wife is entitled to one sixth of the property if there are children in the family but if there are no children, the wife is entitled to one third.

Fac: What does the law says? Who does the property belong to after a person has died?

Law: In the law we have what is called the Will and Inheritance Act which explains how the property of a person who has passed away is supposed to distributed. First of all there is supposed to be an investigation as to whether the person who has died left a will or not. If a will is available and it explains how the deceased wished his or her property to be distributed, the beneficiaries are supposed to go and get consent to implement what was written in the will. Secondly if there is no will left behind, the property will be distributed to the beneficiaries depending on who has died.

Within a matrilineal society, if the man dies and he leaves a wife, children and relatives, the law says all the household property is supposed to be given to the wife. From the remaining things, the wife and children are entitled two fifths. Then the relatives of the man are entitled to the remaining three fifths. If it is the mother who has died, the law says the children are entitled to the property.

The people who get married at the Registrar General have different guidelines to those who get married traditionally. The law says regardless of whether it is the husband or wife who has died, the property is supposed to be left to the surviving spouse and children.

Fac: You have mentioned that all the household property should be left for the wife and children but the rest of the property can be distributed amongst the other relatives. Please give us examples of this property.

Law: The property to be distributed can be the one which was used by the family to generate income such as grocery stores, mini buses, or cars. Household furniture is what is in the house, for example the lounge suite, buckets and kitchen ware. This property is not supposed to be given to anyone besides the widow so she can look after her children properly.

Fac: So if the man left grocery stores, a mini bus, a car, these are supposed to be distributed and the widow and children are entitled to two fifths and the deceased man's relatives are entitled to three fifths.

Now we would like to know why we say it is *nkhanza* take property away from the bereaved. I will ask the T/A why this is so?

T/A: Before we continue we should remember that *nkhanza* is on both sides. Both men and women can be perpetrators. Property grabbing is considered *nkhanza* because the bereaved will be left with nothing since they depended on the deceased.

Sheikh: We already mentioned that in accordance with Islam, an orphan is a very young child who can not look after himself or herself. So if the parent, who provided for him or her, dies, the orphaned children can not work in the fields or do any business to make money for their upkeep. Children have various needs; they need education, food, clothes and other necessities. So if someone else who is not entitled to the inheritance comes and takes the property, this is *nkhunza* because the child will not be able to go to school, will not be able to eat proper. Therefore, God instructed that they are entitled to whatever wealth remains. Furthermore, a person who is entitled to a share of the property should take his or her entitlement and not more because this will also be *nkhanza*.

Law: I would just like to comment on what the Sheikh said. He said if there is lack of honesty or fairness on the distribution of wealth, the beneficiaries end up having economic problems and these may lead to psychological problems. A parent may be troubled thinking of what he or she can do to get school fees, uniforms and food for the children. These problems may force the remaining parent to think of other ways to make money for the children. We all know that for a mother, most of the times the quickest way one can make money is through prostitution. So a mother can think that if she stays with a particular man she may get some maize flour and relish or money to buy food for her children. We all know that prostitution or unprotected sexual intercourse is one way that a person can get infected with AIDS.

T/A: I agree with the previous comment. I know that *nkhanza* does bring about this problem but I feel the biggest problem we have in the villages is poverty which makes most of the women have adulterous affairs even some girls are guilty of immorality. They go out and sleep with men so that they can get money for soap and other necessities and so when they do this they risk getting infected with AIDS. The parents may try and stop them but most of them do not listen. They continue with the immoral behaviour.

Fac: My last question is who is supposed to distribute a deceased person's property?

Law: In this country, the District Commissioner has the power to distribute property that is worth K 20 000.00 or less.

Fac: Are there any questions.

Question: My question goes to the representative for the law. It has been mentioned that if a man dies, all his property is supposed to be inherited by his wife and children. Is it not possible that when the man dies, the property should be distributed equally between the female and male side so as to prevent incidents whereby the woman kills her husband in order to inherit everything?

Law: What we said was the wife and children are entitled to two fifths of the property. Three fifths go to the deceased relatives. What solely belongs to her and the children is the household furniture but business and any other property will be divided between the relatives of the deceased and the wife and children. So the women here should be warned that they should not go out there and kill their husbands with the intention of inheriting everything.

Question: My question is: it seems that the discussion that has been held here concerns those who are wealthy. What if a man and wife are farmers and they grow maize and groundnuts and they harvest three bags. If the husband should die, is there any need to distribute the maize and groundnuts?

Law: In short what we can say is harvested crops are not part pf household furniture so they need to be distributed to the deceased man's relatives and his widow and children. For example, if there were five bags, then the wife and children will get two bags and the relatives get three bags.

Question: My question goes to the lawyer. If a woman gets married to a man who does not own anything and they later divorce. He remarries and then he becomes wealthy. Upon his death are the children from the first wife entitled to anything?

Law: The law says that if a parent dies, all the children whether they are from his current or former marriage are all entitled to a share of his property because the children are innocent beings. They do not take part in encouraging their parents to divorce or become polygamists.

Question: My question goes to the lawyer. You said the wife is entitled to two fifths of the property excluding the household goods and the relatives of the deceased are entitled to three fifths. What if there are only two minibuses or there is a store, how can they share this property? I would also like to know what if the deceased left only property but did not save any money, where would the wife get money to pay for her children's fees?

Law: At the District Commissioner, qualified people are sent out who go and evaluate the property. Maybe the store is worth K 100 000.00, the mini bus K 200 000.00, so in total the property is worth K 300 000.00. The beneficiaries are told the value and they are given a choice of perhaps giving the wife and children the store since they are entitled to less and the relatives of the deceased can take the mini bus. The beneficiaries may choose to have money instead, so they may sell the property and divide the proceeds.

You also asked who would pay the fees of school going children. That will depend on whatever property is left. If there is property that has been left to the mother and children, they may sell some of it to pay the school fees.

Question: What I wanted to know is when it comes to land, how you would define it, is it part of the property that is for distribution.

My other question is if there are no children in the marriage and the husband and wife do not have any living relatives but they both have property. In the event that they both die, who inherits the property?

Law: There are two categories of landholding. Some land is bought, other land is given. If the land belonged to the deceased then it is part of the property that has to be distributed. Then there is land that you ask the chief for or land that belongs to your family or tribe that is used for farming. When the spouse dies, that land goes back to the people who gave it to him or her. What the bereaved can take are seedlings or harvest.

Regarding the question of when there are no beneficiaries left, then the property goes to the government but only after a thorough investigation has been carried out and no living relatives can be identified.

Question: My question is what do you do when all the household property is taken from the widow by the relatives of the man?

Law: The first thing that should be done is that the issue should be taken to people who are close to you such as the chief. If the chief sees that what he has instructed is not being followed then the case should be forwarded to a court of law. Once in court if there is evidence that indeed there was wrong doing and the household property has been taken from the wife unlawfully these people can be arrested and sentenced to prison for five years or pay a fine of K 20 000.00.

Question: The woman has been found guilty of practising witchcraft on her husband with the purpose inheriting all the property. The relatives of the man find out that she went to a witchdoctor to get potions to kill her husband. So when the man dies, his relatives know why he died. In such a situation, will the wife get any of the property?

Sheikh: I will try and answer your question. When it comes to witchcraft, we have one problem: It is very hard to prove that it was committed. When it comes to religion, life and death are considered to be God given.

Question: My question is for the lawyer. A man marries a woman and she goes and lives with him at his home village. He builds a house and they live harmoniously but unfortunately the husband dies. Now, who owns the house since that may be the only house that was built in the family? Can his relatives chase her away and tell her to go back to her village, arguing that the man built the house?

Law: As we said earlier, when you acquire property together it belongs to both people in the marriage. The house was built with the intention of the couple living together there. In the event of the husband's death, his widow has the right to continue living in that house. But the woman has no right to bring other men into that house. That would make his relatives very unhappy and go against her to the extent of chasing her away. If the woman stays there and does not bring other men and also looks after her in-laws I am sure her late husband's relatives will not chase her away.

Question: We belong to a matrilineal society. So when the wife dies, what can the man do if her relatives say he should leave their home? He has made investments there and considers the place where he lived with his wife his home?

T/A: The way I understand our culture is that if the wife dies, the husband should not be chased away but should be allowed to stay and look after his children. If anyone chases him away he should go to the Magistrate's Court and file a complaint.

Law: It seems that the property was accumulated by the husband and the deceased wife. If her relatives want him to go back to his home, they should follow appropriate procedures to make sure he gets what he is entitled to.

Conclusion

All three panellists agree that property grabbing is unacceptable. They differ on who should get how much after the death of a spouse, but all agree that the surviving spouse and the children should receive the main share and the relatives of the deceased a smaller one.

Islam considers the orphans as main heirs

According to the **law**, the household property should go to the widow; from the remaining items she and the children are entitled to two fifths while the relatives to the husband should receive three fifths.

The **T/A** does not give a clear statement on who should get how much, but he points out that the division of the property should be done fairly during the customary ceremony. During that ceremony the relatives from both sides should consider that both spouses have been working to achieve the assets in the home. Therefore, the widow or widower should remain with what he or she has been working for.

Anybody who takes more than what he or she is entitled to is acting against the law (customary or constitutional) and there can be no justification for this.

The effects of property grabbing are numerous:

On the immediate family
The sudden loss of property and other resources is economically devastating, usually leaving the surviving spouse unable to support their children or themselves. Widows and children may engage in high risk behaviour like prostitution to earn a living. This makes them vulnerable to abuse by their 'clients' and to HIV infection.

Children are forced to drop out of school. Some are driven to beg in the streets. This makes them vulnerable to sexual abuse and HIV/Aids infection.

Where a widower is chased away in matrilineal areas, he has to find resources to start again despite the fact that he may be very old.

Property grabbing leaves people feeling helpless and hopeless. It seriously damages their spirit at a time when they are most vulnerable. Many victims feel like slaves who worked hard to get property that others now enjoy. Therefore, it can lead to mental illnesses like depression.

Effect on the community

Property grabbing leads to the complete breakdown of relations between the surviving spouse, children, and the deceased's relatives. This can affect others in their village – for example, relatives and friends of the person chased away or whose property was grabbed might also start fighting with each other.

Sometimes the loss of all of their property drives people to crime. Not only is this bad for the community, but it could also lead to imprisonment for the offender, further destroying their family.

References

Baumgart M., Moran G.; Lekani Nkhanza Training Manual, Zomba 2006

Saur M., Semu L., Hauya S.; Nkhanza, Listening to people's voice, Zomba 2005

Soeger, A. et al.; Gender-based Violence, Conflict Management and Sharia, Mangochi, Frankfurt 2004

The Constitution of the Republic of Malawi; Malawi Government, 2000

The Holy Qur'an, translated by M. H. Shakir, Tahrike Tarsile Qur'an Inc., 1983